To Nadi

May God bless and
keep you always.
Aubrey I. Lynch

THE SACRED HEART LEGACY

SOUL OF A CITY

By

Aubrey J. Lynch

authorHOUSE™

1663 LIBERTY DRIVE, SUITE 200
BLOOMINGTON, INDIANA 47403
(800) 839-8640
WWW.AUTHORHOUSE.COM

First published by AuthorHouse 07/12/05

ISBN: 1-4208-4719-8 (sc)
ISBN: 1-4208-4720-1 (dj)

Printed in the United States of America
Bloomington, Indiana

This book is printed on acid-free paper.

THE BISHOP'S INTRODUCTION

Over the years, on various occasions, I have had the opportunity to introduce people at public events or to introduce a book to the reading public.

To introduce this book, *The Sacred Heart Legacy*, I consider a truly unique privilege. I am honored by the invitation and only hope that I can do justice to the task.

Perhaps you have read books in the past detailing the history of a parish or a diocese. There are many of them in circulation. I assure you, most of them are so lacking in conveying a Spirit-life that they can make a reader conclude that history is always going to be dry and boring. Most histories of parish churches or dioceses are filled with details about the clergy, bishops or priests, who have been part of the Church life over the span of time covered by the historical record. Often, the major achievements detailed in the book will be the succession of buildings that were constructed under the guidance of the pastor or bishop. Or, you might find a lot of numbers – baptisms, first communions, marriages and funerals and so on.

This book is different. It sets forth in an honest, even critical way, the dynamic life of a "community of disciples of Jesus." You will not find out a lot about when the cornerstone was laid for this building. Nor will you get a long list of pastors who put up buildings or were chaplains to the ladies' guild or guided the ushers' club and the like.

Instead, you will read the personal stories of the individual people who have come to be Sacred Heart Parish.

I suppose that it is only fair to alert prospective readers that the history of this community is the history of an African-American Catholic community. For this reason it is inevitably a tiny piece of the history of racism in the Catholic Church in the United States. As you get to know the people of Sacred Heart Church, you will feel indignation and sorrow, I hope, at the ugly sin of white racism in the Catholic Church. Those who witness in this book to the suffering and humiliations they have experienced at the hands of white people and especially white leadership at every level in the Church, do so without bitterness or hatred. Their ability to follow the way of Jesus in returning love for hate and good for evil is one of the most inspiring elements of their story.

And even though the racism in the Church goes on, they manifest a commitment to the Catholic tradition as theirs, a commitment nothing will shake or weaken. These are people who can sing with greater authenticity than most, "We've come this far by faith..." and that faith will be forever the real cornerstone of this community as it moves on into new phases of their life as a parish.

One final reason why I am pleased to introduce this book and urge many people to read it is the timeliness of its publication. In the Archdiocese of Detroit we have already gone through a very painful period of closing churches and suppressing parishes. We are currently in the process of developing a so-called strategic plan for the diocese. Anyone with eyes to see recognizes immediately that the plan's development and implementation will result in the closing of many more churches, especially in the City of Detroit. An honest look at what has happened and what will happen leads to a tremendous sadness in the soul of anyone who loves the Church and wants it to be the kind of community Jesus founded – a community that reaches out in love to all, regardless of race or economic situation. In fact, to be genuinely true to the vision of Jesus, it would be a Church which made a preferential option for those oppressed by the sin of racism or the sin of economic oppression. Instead, we have a situation where the Catholic Church in Detroit is abandoning the city. The message is clear: We really do not care much about an African-American presence in the Catholic Church, nor do we care very much about the poor.

When you read this book detailing the history and legacy of this beautiful community of Jesus' disciples located in the heart of the city of Detroit, you will see with astonishing clarity how different it could be. Sacred Heart Church is the model for making the Catholic Church of the Archdiocese of Detroit a Church of the city and for the City of Detroit at this point in Detroit's history.

With or without the support of those who lead the Archdiocese, the people of Sacred Heart will carry on. As they conclude their story, so it will be:

> "We have been deeply affected
> by our examination of this
> congregation. We have learned
> a great deal that will aid
> us in our continuing efforts
> to tell the tales of the Black
> Diaspora.
> We sincerely pray that this
> record of our findings will
> somehow repay the congregation
> and its leader for giving us the
> honor of the telling.
> Deo Gratias."

Bishop Thomas Gumbleton
Archdiocese of Detroit

Background:

Bishop Thomas Gumbleton is the pastor of St. Leo's parish in the inner city of Detroit, Michigan. He was ordained to the Priesthood on June 2nd 1956.

Recognition: Bishop Gumbleton is the founding president of Pax Christi USA (1972-1991), former president of Bread for the World (1976-84) and co-founder of the Michigan Coalition for Human Rights (1980). He has been a board member of numerous organizations including the MK Gandhi institute of Non-violence, New Ways Ministry, Witness for Peace, and the Fellowship of Reconciliation. He has received numerous awards for his actions on behalf of peace and justice including the Pax Christi USA Pope Paul VI Teacher of Peace Award (1991) and Call To Action's Leadership Award (1995). He was bestowed the University of Notre Dame Peacemaker award in 1991. In 1997 he was awarded the National Peace Foundation Award of Peacemaker/Peacebuilder in Washington, D.C.

FOREWORD

History always begins with a question. The historian is the one who searches for the answer. A little over fifty years ago, black Catholics began to ask, "Where did the history of black Catholics in America begin?" Some said that it was impossible to answer. The documents had long since been destroyed. Much information had not been recorded. Others said we did not have the tools to find the answer. Still, many more said that, on the contrary, the only thing needed was the will to dig a little deeper and to look a little harder. The tools were there; we just needed to use them.

Aubrey Lynch, a parishioner of Sacred Heart Church in Detroit, has presented us an historical study of his parish church. This is a history told us in a new and vivid way. Not confining himself to a traditional parish history centered on the pastors, the assistants, and the sisters in the school; he has sought to tell the history of a people and a population—the laity as well as the priests, the religious as well as the students—all within the time span of a very tumultuous period. It is the story of an immigrant people who were replaced by a migrant minority people. It is the story of how a parish of German Catholics became a parish of African American Catholics. It is the presentation of a Catholic parish living through the Paschal Mystery of death and new life. Aubrey Lynch has recounted this history with passion and conviction; in doing so has added to the increasing store of black Catholic history.

The legacy of Sacred Heart was forged on the battleground of social change and racial strife. Controversy has been present in every period of this parish's development. It is not surprising that some of the author's judgments and conclusions will not be shared by everyone. Nor is it surprising that the dispassionate treatment of the detached scholar is not always apparent in this volume. Yet, the author has sought to portray with great sympathy the various personages who played an important role in the history of Sacred Heart. A real effort has been made, moreover, to rely upon the collective memory of the church members. Interweaving the personal recollections with the historical account itself, the interviews have become like the chorus sustaining the drama. As a result the oral history as well as the letters and the documents of the parish archives, the archdiocesan archives; and the Felician Sisters Archives have provided a solid basis for a well written parish history.

Daniel Rudd (1854-1933), the black Catholic lay leader at the end of the nineteenth century, who organized the black Catholic lay congresses from 1889 to 1894, also published a black Catholic weekly newspaper, *The American Catholic Tribune.* First published in Cincinnati from 1888 to 1894 and then in Detroit from 1894 to about 1899—at that time there were indeed very few black Catholics in Detroit—Rudd insisted in his editorials that the black Catholic community had the "mission" to be a "leaven" for their fellow black Americans and a "bearer" for their race. The people of Sacred Heart Church in Detroit have been just that…the leaven for the black community and the bearer of their race.

Cyprian Davis, O.S.B.
Saint Meinrad Archabbey
Lent, 2005

Background:

Father Cyprian Davis has written numerous books and articles in the area of monastic history and the history and spirituality of African American Catholics in the United States. In 1990 he published "The History of Black Catholics in the United States." (New York: Crossroad), which received the John Gilmary Shea Award in 1991.

In 1994-1995, he served as a visiting professor of Church history at the Monastic Studium established in West Africa at the Abbey of Dzogbégan in Togo and the Abbey of Koubri in Burkina Faso. He was as visiting professor at the Abbey of Keur Moussa in Senegal in 1995-1996, and at the Benedictine and Trappist monasteries in Nigeria in 1997-1998. He also has lectured on the development of monastic archives in monasteries of men and women in Benin, Burkina Faso, Ivory Coast, Senegal, and Togo in West Africa.

Davis is a longtime scholar and monk of St. Meinrad Archabbey. He was professed in 1951 and was ordained to the priesthood in 1956. He received a licentiate of sacred theology degree from The Catholic University of America in 1957, and a doctorate in history at the University of Louvain in Belgium in 1977.

ACKNOWLEDGMENTS

Myriad tasks must be accomplished from the time that an idea is voiced, until a finished product is presented. That is very true about this book. The idea began with the Sacred Heart Book Club in May of 2003. Since that day, many people have contributed various amounts of time, energy and expertise.

The Sacred Heart books referred to as "archives" had been assembled by Dolores Comeaux-Taylor and Patricia A. Turner.

Barbara Hunt, Sacred Heart Alumni Chairperson, Joyce Townsend, Jamil Allah and Maxine Adams provided valuable historical documentation and input.

The Felician Sisters welcomed us to their motherhouse in Livonia and shared many stories from their memories and from their archives.

Willie Bell Gibson and Patt Van Dyke critiqued an early draft.

Bishop Thomas Gumbleton was gracious in answering our request to write the Introduction to the book.

Father Cyprian Davis offered several very valuable ideas to improve readability and accuracy as well as writing the Foreword. We gained a great deal from his diligence and scholarship.

We are exceedingly grateful for the support that Father Norman Thomas has provided throughout this project.

The following people also participated in some way. It may have been attendance at one meeting or several. It may have been interviewing, recording, researching, reviewing, or encouraging others to do these tasks. Whatever the contribution, large or small, the book was made possible with the help of these people:

Judy Carty, Connie Daldin, Margaret Davis, Hugh Day, Pauline George, Johnie Gilmore, Dolores Harold, Mary Ann Humphries, Mary Hutchinson, Ann Kraemer, Carole Lasker, Anne Sullivan Smith, Barbara Hughes Smith, Sandra Richardson Smith, Clarence

Street, Angela Tarrant-Cook, Steve Tate, Michaela Terrell, John Thorne, Almeta White, Peggy Williams, Gloria Wright.

It "takes a village to raise a child" and it takes a whole community to write, painstakingly, its own history.

Thank you to everyone who worked on this book. We give special thanks to all those who have lived, and are continuing to live, the "Legacy" of The Sacred Heart of Jesus Catholic Church.

Carole Lasker
For The Sacred Heart Book Committee

TABLE OF CONTENTS

TIMELINE

1875	A group of German American Catholics, with the help of Father Aloysius Kurtz, O.F.M., received permission from Bishop Casper Borgess to establish Sacred Heart of Jesus Church at Prospect (Rivard) and Grove (Eliot).
1876	The church and school were dedicated on July 16th with Father Eugene Butterman as the first pastor.
1911	On September 1st, a group of 18 black Catholics, with the help of Father Joseph Wuest, C .S. Sp., began St. Peter Claver Church in a large classroom of St. Mary School in downtown Detroit.
1914	On Thanksgiving Day, Father Wuest led the group to a small Episcopal Church on Beaubien and Eliot with Father Charles Kapp, C. S. Sp. as the new pastor. That church became St. Peter Claver.
1932	Father Henry Thiefels became pastor.
1936	The school began in the apartment house which was also the rectory. There were 64 students.
1938	On September 1st, the congregation marched to their new home at Sacred Heart of Jesus Church. There were 1500 members. St. Peter Claver was closed.
1941	The first freshman class started.
1943	There was a Race riot in Detroit for 36 hours.
1945	Forty-five students were in the first graduating class. There were 550 students in grades one - twelve.

1957	The High School closed in June.
1965	The Grade School closed.
1967	The school building became an alcoholic rehabilitation center until 1972.
1968	Father Stegman, C. S. Sp., was transferred and Father Norman Thomas became pastor.
1973	The school building was torn down.
1980	The Activities Building was added.
2004	2379 parishioners, 1327 families

John Lynch

PROLOGUE

We are tellers of tales. We are descended from the griots of western Africa, those who have kept the story of our people alive. We can no longer depend on memory and our very fruitful oral traditions. In the modern age we must write if we are to reach our ever-expanding audience. We want to relate to you the story of a remarkable Catholic parish that parallels, with astounding precision, the development of our people in the United States. From its humble, even obscure origins, to its current powerful impact on a major city, this parish sings the beautiful song of how a resourceful and patient people survive and prosper under incredibly hostile conditions. We represent the spirit of the early tellers of tales by focusing on the history of a unique village-like group of worshippers. The congregation is that of the Sacred Heart of Jesus, a parish in the heart of Detroit, Michigan. Those familiar with the church just call it Sacred Heart.

The story we will tell is a continuing story. We relate it now because change is inevitable. The changes we foresee will determine whether the influence of Sacred Heart Church will intensify, may God make it so, or if it will fade away. We have been watching over this phenomenon for close to seven decades now. Even after all of this time the church is still looking pretty good, considering all that it has been through. The things that have happened there would fill quite a number of volumes if we could capture all of it. There have been baptisms and first communions, weddings, and funerals, too, many to count, but each one has a story behind it. There have been many, many parties and happy times, but there have been quarrels, too, and real knockdown fights. We have seen the city change around this great institution from white to black and now there's quite a mixture, both inside and out. We must say that we are really proud of what has been accomplished here. It certainly reflects well on the accomplishments of African Americans and, God willing, it portends great things for the future. We know that God remains with us so we try to reduce our anxiety for the future. We want to tell you, as clearly as we can, using Sacred Heart as a sterling example, where we African Americans have been and where we appear to be going. We shall do so with the help of the voices of the congregation so that you will know how we have been able to carry on. There is so much to tell. Please bear with us as we go. We griots have been at this for centuries now and our age begins to betray us at times.

INTRODUCTION

Sacred Heart Church, located at the corner of Eliot and Rivard in Detroit, Michigan, was solemnly dedicated on the 16th of July 1876. As is customary, it was built as the parish home of Detroit's German community. By "customary," we mean that most parish churches were and are built to serve the needs of a particular ethnic group. We make a point of this because this practice has been known to cause at least some misunderstanding, and in too many cases, even conflict and bitterness among ethnic groups, to our eternal mortification. We will trace some of the history of the Germans because their contribution was so important to the success of the African American congregation that ultimately filled the church.

Sacred Heart – The German Church

We are hard pressed to restrain our admiration as we reflect on the original German congregation. They were entirely devoted to their parish and worked desperately hard to nurture and develop their church. Information we have about their attitudes comes from documents still available in the church archives that contain their own writing of their history. Consequently, we are privileged to eavesdrop as they express their deep and abiding love for the church they built for themselves.

> "The people of the parish were mostly good and zealous Catholics willing to do their share also financially, as far as they were able. As it happens, there were some who would rather shirk their duty. During the first house collection I took up, I collected 50 cents on one whole street of considerable length, which did not go very far towards paying of $28,000. Some that lived between St. Mary's and Sacred Heart churches would not go to Sacred Heart although they belonged there. One lady told me that she would not go to the woods. ("In den Busch; da gehe ich nicht hinaus.") Some people did even more than one could reasonably expect of them. I remember one parishioner having a family with several children, earning $11.00 a week, who contributed for church and school purposes

about $39.00 a year."

Sacred Heart Archives[1]

This remarkable statement reveals so much. In one paragraph we discover that:

- Many people, of whatever nationality, are reluctant to contribute to the Church. What is the source of this ambivalence?
- A parish activist felt comfortable asking everyone in the neighborhood to contribute. Why have neighborhoods become so much less cohesive?
- Sacred Heart was "in the woods." The current setting shows how far we are removed from that time.
- One devoted family person made a huge sacrifice to support the church. How does such a family maintain its reliance on the efficacy of the Church and the Word?

We have posed the questions to indicate the differences between a time long past and the present day. Those of us who reside in the US are embedded in a time period that is fraught with angst and portent as well as an increasing undercurrent of fear. Other areas of the world are long past angst. Subject to US hegemony, they suffer under the jackboots of arrogance and greed. African Americans have long known the impact of both. Bear this in mind as our story continues. In this story we will look to the lessons of Sacred Heart to find a way out of the morass.

There have been some radical changes in the fabric of the US since the rather innocent time implicit in the documents of the Sacred Heart archives. Let us examine another reference for what it can

---

[1] The Sacred Heart Archives contain numerous documents. However, a great many are undated and are collected in loose-leaf binders with no clear or consistent organizing principle. Consequently, they cannot be referenced in the way normally expected by scholars. Those who would like to see the documents would have to make arrangements with the Pastor at the Sacred Heart Rectory.

tell us about the relationship of the parish to the community at that time.

> "The spirit of harmonious fellowship and mutual encouragement obtaining in those days among the people found a beautiful expression in the splendid turnout which graced the occasion of the laying of the cornerstone (Sunday, June 27, 1875). The line of march commenced at Michigan Avenue, down Adams and St. Antoine to the location of the new church, corner of Grove and Prospect Streets. It consisted of three divisions. The first division was headed by the Marshalls, a platoon of city police, Detroit National Guard Band, Saarfield, Independent Zouaves, Westphalian Shooting club, the Hibernians, St. Vincent's School Society, the Christian Doctrine Society of St. Vincent's Parish, two branches of Fr. Matthew's Total Abstinence Society and the Guild Society."
>
> Sacred Heart Archives

The writer goes on to describe in detail the participants in the two other divisions that took part in the parade. We are impressed, as the writer is impressed, by the wide variety of participants, the sheer number of organizations and the fact that the City of Detroit chose to participate by sending a platoon of city police. This description shows how important a Catholic parish church was to the neighborhood and to the city. The writer then describes the church and its interior.

"Sacred Heart Church is an imposing structure, built of brick, having a length of 125 feet and breadth of 54 feet with a seating capacity of 1,000 persons.   Built in roman style, it presents a friendly appearance and is an ornament of the surrounding locality. The slender tower rests upon a quadrangular base of brick supporting an eight-cornered wooden super-structure, ends in a pyramidal peak, holding aloft the symbol of salvation, a sturdy sentinel of Teuton piety, standing guard over city and country, a lasting witness to the faith and generosity of German catholicity.

"The interior of the church is very pleasing and devotional. The main altar artistically built, impresses the beholder with its slender forms."

Sacred Heart Archives

First Communion in Sacred Heart, the German Church, 1938

The love that the writer bears for the church is obvious even in this brief statement. The writer goes on to describe in even more reverent detail the stained glass windows and the statues, along with their donors. We were greatly affected by the revelation that the stained glass window representing the Guardian Angel with Child was the gift of the school children.

The document from which these descriptions were taken was prepared to defend the church against a proposed takeover by people of Italian descent. It continues to build its case in support of the Germans by describing the intentions of its first pastor, Reverend Father Eugene Butterman, O. F. M. (Franciscan Order).

> "Realizing the need of strong hands in bringing order out of chaos, he (Father Butterman) strictly insisted upon his parishioners learning and observing the rules of orderly procedure in the transaction of parochial affairs. The apparently strict enforcement of the regulations he found necessary at times, impressed itself emphatically upon the character of the parish and enabled it to remain steadfastly upon the path of law and obedience to legitimate authority, when the days of trial arose."
>
> Sacred Heart Archives

This passage shows how important the pastor is to the direction of the church. Father Butterman's leadership molded the character of Sacred Heart for much of its early history. The writer then gives an elaborate account of the successors to Father Butterman and of the organizations and people that gave the church its life. The document was written to show how much effort the parish and its pastor had to deliver to ensure the success of the parish. It ended with a plea to the bishop to consider this glorious history and leave the church in German hands. Ultimately, much to the joy of the later African Americans, the plea was successful for only a brief time.

Much as we treasure the devotion and solid contributions of the German parishioners, our story is really about the black people, African Americans, who found refuge within those walls and remained to provide the achievements of which we speak. Consequently, we shall not dwell on the original flock or even on the structure and design of this lovely edifice. The church still stands. Those who wish to see for themselves are quite welcome to come view the classic lines, elegant spire and stained glass. These are the kind of details that could make any parish proud. A statement from Father Norman Thomas, the current pastor, brings us back to reality.

"The story of a church is not its buildings; it is of the people who built it, and why they did it. It is a story of many people – their births, their living, their schooling, their marrying, and their dying. Lives touch here; dreams, joys and sorrows are shared and celebrated. Here the Spirit moves to comfort the distressed to strengthen the courageous, to uplift the depressed, to provoke the listless, to set on fire, to light the way. It is the story of people failing, praying, singing, laughing, crying, changing, struggling, rising."

Father Norman Thomas

Father Thomas certainly describes what we believe to be true. To be sure, once we focused on Sacred Heart as a vibrant part of the community, we came to know many different kinds of people. They have often amazed us with their constant striving, their numerous conflicts and their ultimate survival in the face of enormous odds. True enough, the Germans built Sacred Heart and thrived here for a time. But, as the black people became more numerous, the Germans began to withdraw, leaving the church in a bit of distress. The truth, unthinkable as it is, was that the church indeed was faced with premature abandonment, possibly death. Instead, praise God, an energetic, oppressed people who valued the sanctuary that the church provided, revived it. They sought a place where they could worship Our Lord and Savior, He for whom the church was named. They desired to live in peace and among like-minded, similarly oppressed people. The story we tell is of these people, their warmth, pain, love, sorrows and joys. As a result of this blessing from God, the name, Sacred Heart, has become synonymous with social activism. The name is also synonymous with "welcoming community of believers." The name is now one of relevance and influence in an historical city that has its own crosses to bear. The name bears such relevance because of the people it serves…a wide variety of people, mainly African Americans, but inclusive of all who share the vision, the vision of those who believe in the salvation of the Word.

The Sacred Heart Legacy

Sacred Heart has come to this point by offering a disciplined path to righteousness. Oh no, there is no "how-to" manual. We are not yet convinced that any one person in the parish can tell us precisely the path that makes Sacred Heart so unique. What we mean is this. We have observed over more than seven decades that those who have been most influential in this congregation are those who live the Word. Just as Christ has said to us, one road that we might follow is broad, straight and comfortable. Another road is overgrown, twisting with no clear signposts. To follow the second road requires courage, perseverance and a degree of faith that will test the hardiest of souls.

Sacred Heart is living testimony that those who follow the second path are rewarded many times over in ways that are almost unfathomable. The riches are, indeed, not of this world, but certainly in it. While there are wealthy people in Sacred Heart, it is not wealth that distinguishes this parish. Quite the contrary, status, power and the like are not the blessings that God bestows on these people as their reward even though many of its members have had, and still have these things.

The legacy is far more valuable than trinkets and illusions.

We consider ourselves privileged to relate this story because in defining the Sacred Heart legacy and getting your understanding and agreement to our interpretation, we hope to unravel a mystery. Where is one to find peace, solace and comfort in a world tearing itself apart in greed, hatred and violence? Many people are able to say the words, "God is the answer." True rewards come to those who live the meaning of that statement. Believers know this to be true. But we hope to speak to other than the choir.

We think we can show you that what is happening in this small, powerful community of Sacred Heart can be a model that can be replicated, not by rote, but by trial and example. When we understand how Sacred Heart came to be what it is, we will see the infinity of God's wisdom and holy plan.

Trust in the Lord and He will make a way.

Follow the Word and He will not lead you astray.

The Sacred Heart legacy is that past and present members are living witnesses to that truth.

Voices of the Congregation

We are fascinated by the fact that members of the parish do not dwell on the difficulties. They rejoice at having found a home. Rejoicing in gifts from God is a central element in the legacy. They, themselves, are often puzzled by references to the struggle. For them, the crucial fact is that they are an active, influential and effective community composed of many different types of people. We dare say that most members would be puzzled by the very term, "legacy," as it applies to their beloved church and its leader. It is we, the tellers of tales, who draw meaning and significance from the path that the congregation traveled. The members of the parish have found a degree of peace and enjoyment in each other that allows them to demonstrate, without reflection, what it means to be a Christian community.

We can give you a better understanding of what it means to be a part of Sacred Heart today by allowing you to listen to what its members have to say.[2]

The McCauley family is representative of those stalwarts who have been a part of Sacred Heart for generations. What they have to say gives us a way to move gently into the heart of our story.

> My parents were not Catholic when they arrived. My father was in the drama club and got connected to Catholics that way. They were involved in concerts with Kelvin Ventour and several of them were at Sacred Heart.
>
> My dad became Catholic before he married. He brought my mother into the church.
>
> Mary McCauley Cosey
>
> Sacred Heart offered a lot of what dad needed. He received a lot of support from Father Thiefels. When my mother died, he

---

[2]   The statements from the parishioners were taken from interviews conducted in 2004.

People who left have decided to come back. They brought their
children and grands.

The kids hear and see the history of their parents and
grandparents. The pictures and plaques attest to that history.
The kids like that.

Anthony McCauley

The poignancy of this story is almost lost in the matter of fact way in
which it is offered. When the McCauley patriarch, Jesse McCauley,
Sr. became a member of the Sacred Heart parish about 1936, black
people were in the midst of exceedingly difficult hardships. The
family was in desperate need of help. Father Thiefels and the Church
answered the call. Clearly, the family has never forgotten and has
never ceased to be grateful. "The kids hear and see the history…the
kids like that." The gratitude is transmitted through the generations
along with the devotion…and the adherence to the Word.

The McCauley family gives us a hint as to the source of the Sacred
Heart legacy…a welcoming church and its dedicated priests and
nuns.

The following, rather stirring tribute shows one of the ways in which
Sacred Heart became so important in the lives of its parishioners.

I have friends who are family (not blood relatives) that have
been a part of my life since 1945 when the dedicated, teaching
Felician nuns accepted me into the 4th grade class at the only all
"Negro", affordable and accepting Catholic school in Detroit.

Sister Lucille was then the Principal and Father Henry Thiefels, the Pastor. Of course I could never forget Sister Mansueta, Sister Calesantia and Sister Alfreda. Then there were our great dances in the basement of the school, where Edward Daniels exhibited his unique moves; the debate team, school plays and trips; the 1953 Parish Ball where the crowning of the Parish Queen, sponsored by Father Dooley was a highlight.

Our three story brick school building stood on the corner of Rivard and Eliot across the street from the church and rectory. A block west of us was Hastings Street (that is a story in itself). A block east was Russell public school. And about 4 blocks west was St. Peter Claver Settlement House that complemented much of the character building that Sacred Heart provided. In elementary school, many of us went to St. Peter Claver after school for social and club activities, sports and homework assistance. Parents were very involved at both Sacred Heart and St. Peter Claver whenever possible (most of our parents worked).

I came to Sacred Heart because my family believed that a good education was mandatory and a given. I was born in Mississippi (but our family came from Louisiana, Virginia and Texas) with a legacy of Black History, education as a priority, family/ personal responsibility and perseverance. There was never any question that I would go on to college. My grandfather was a master craftsman of fine furniture, my grandmother taught piano and organ and my great-great aunt taught until she was in her 90's, (she put her age back each year after 70), my mom was a seamstress, domestic worker, waitress, housewife, community and school volunteer and wonderful mom.

Morning Mass before class, the caring attitudes of the nuns and priests, the curriculum and taps on the knuckles were the tools used at Sacred Heart to promote the consciousness, determination, self-discipline and resolution necessary for the world of work and the resiliency to overcome barriers. Those years of Latin classes continue to enrich my pronunciation and use of English and the learning of other languages.

Sacred Heart school exuded an environment of cleanliness. We had dark wood floors that always looked as if they had just been waxed. Guess what? They were waxed 2 to 3 times weekly, but not by some janitor or fancy machine. Students brought the packaging from loaves of bread to school. Reuse and Recycle is nothing new! Wonder Bread wrapping contained a thick

xxxiii

coating of wax. After school or sometimes as a break, students put those bread bags over their feet and we slid side to side from one end of the halls to the other. Et Voila!! Beautiful floors. No, no one considered that to be child labor or unfair practices. It was exercise, fun, teamwork, interaction, work ethics, friendship building and ownership in our shared space.

I still belong to Sacred Heart because most of the legacy there continues in this different time and some new spaces. For me and my dear Sacred Heart family we feel that our inheritance is precious. The Sacred Heart church family offers the opportunity to promote peace, unity, and holistic self-sufficiency and inspiration to this and future generations.

Barbara J. Williams

This tribute speaks to a number of issues which bear on the place of Sacred Heart in the life of Detroit and, indeed, in the world. Sacred Heart has been, and is, a place that nurtures and develops its parishioners in spite of daunting odds. People who take its values to heart often overcome life obstacles that would crush others who have not had such strengthening experiences.

Another set of tributes shows how leadership plays such an important part in the life of this church.

I have been a Catholic all my life.
But, once I was no longer forced to go to Catholic schools, I chose not to do so.
By the time I got married and started a family, I realized I needed help and started going back to church.
I bounced from church to church.
Then, I decided that I wouldn't be Catholic anymore.
Before I decided to try another denomination, a friend told me, "Before you do that, check out this church called Sacred

Heart."
I brought my husband and my children here for a 10:30 Mass and I was appalled.
"This is not a Catholic church. I don't know what it is."
After I got over the shock, I realized that this is what I had been looking for.
I introduced myself to Father Thomas at the door. When we came back he knew my name, my husband's name and all of my children.
We gave him our phone number.

> He called and we talked about things we might do.
> He called a year later and talked about the things we had agreed
> to do.
> We have been active members ever since.
> We agreed to do those things because of the way he talks to
> you.
>
> > Valerie Watkins

Again we hear from a person, Valerie Watkins, who has a dire need and finds solace at Sacred Heart through the attentions of its leader, Father Norman Thomas. We emphasize her mention of a particular characteristic that is compelling and that is Father Thomas' memory.

> A friend who wanted me to meet Father Thomas invited me
> to Sacred Heart. He said Father Thomas was different. You
> can talk to him and he understands. He is relaxed. What really
> brought me was that I lost my wife who was my childhood
> sweetheart. I found so much comfort, not just in Father T., but
> also in the church. The attitudes, friendliness, openness in the
> church give me comfort.
>
> > Lewis Blount

With Lewis Blount's tribute we begin to get a fuller view of what Sacred Heart means to its parishioners. Again, the leadership is critical, but there is something else, the comforting "attitudes, friendliness and openness" among the church members.

> I was baptized in New Orleans.
> I was in the last 8th grade graduating class at Sacred Heart.
> When I first came back from Chicago I was shocked at how
> the congregation and the neighborhood had declined.
> Then Padre came.
>
> I ran up on Padre who invited me back.
> I became his secretary.
> As Father's secretary he knew a little bit about me.
> I was a History major and Father Thomas suggested that I
> would be much better at Social Work.
> He said, "I am going to be honest with you, as a History
> teacher, you can't remember nothing."

He was right.
Sacred Heart became a place where everybody was welcome.
Those who were not traditionally welcome at other Catholic
churches...mixed marriages, ex-nuns, and ex-priests, people
that just didn't fit anyplace else. Most of all, the service is
reflective of the congregation.
He was not afraid to try new things, such as the street dances.
He is different from any priest I've known.

Lois Johnson

Once more we get a picture of a charismatic leader within a parish
that is welcoming to everyone, including those who would be outcasts
in other places. Clearly, there is something special going on in such
a setting.

We want to use testimonials such as these to show you how parish
members react to their experiences at Sacred Heart. If we are
successful at giving you an encompassing picture of the church,
we feel confident that you will see how a combination of historical
events and human striving has produced a remarkable outcome.
That outcome is so valuable that we would love to see it reproduced
in other places and in future times.

We have undertaken the mission to relate this story to you because we
are growing old now and there are many distractions in the modern
world. Also, the driving force behind this story is vulnerable.
Sacred Heart's pastor, Father Norman Thomas, a good shepherd, is
as subject to God's immutable laws as are we all. We need to tell
this story before we are no longer in a position to do so. We beg the
assistance of God to complete this mission before...

Enough of that. We hope we do not offend by saying that we are
proud of our fortuitous decision to focus on Sacred Heart. We want to
shout to the world that we have achieved our position because of our
own beliefs. We believe it to be important to relate the uniqueness of
the methods by which Sacred Heart has come to this point. If we do
our job effectively, we will preserve the motivation, the spirit, and
the story of a powerful people for future generations.

Let us remind you that many forces operate to prevent this parish
from continuing on its path. It is, after all, part of a large bureaucracy

that is often heedless to all except its own purposes. Memories, on which the parishioners depend, are often unreliable and subject to misinterpretation when filtered through errant perceptions. Most of all, leadership of the kind necessary to help this church make its way in an often chaotic world is rare. We have come to realize how important leadership is to the parishioners because we have seen how Sacred Heart has been blessed with truly exceptional leadership for an inordinately long time.

Please note that the purpose for this work is to preserve the story. The written word will keep memories fresh. We pray that our recounting will help to focus perceptions and appreciate what God has done. With His continuing blessings we will use this recounting to point the way toward the proper path on the journey all must take. We pray that our efforts will encourage the doubtful in the unrelenting struggle to stay on the paths of righteousness for His Namesake.

Our people have had a very difficult time. We cringe at the unremitting hostility directed at black people. However, we are aware that hostilities are directed at the disenfranchised of whatever color. Black people would do well to consider themselves as one with all people who struggle against the cruelties of greed and power. We are as dependent on others who share our difficulties as they are on us. Our destiny is bound together. Thank God that this is so. Our people have known adversity that would make lesser beings give up. We will recount some of the horrors that have befallen us. But, bear in mind, this story is not about the horror, which we all know, but about a people who survived it and now prosper by adhering to the Word.

Much of this work is about historical events that shaped our consciousness and our determination. It will detail the passage from historical antecedents to the first black Catholic congregation in the State of Michigan. It will then follow that congregation as it solidifies its position and gains larger and more permanent houses of worship. It will show how Sacred Heart came to be a part of this remarkable passage and, above all, why its parishioners can be proud to be a part of this history.

This story will be embellished with the voices of those who have contributed to and enjoyed the benefits of the passage. These voices will show the beauty that emerges from adversity, the quiet dignity that results in power and the confident reliance on the Word that overcomes all misfortune. These voices do not specify a plan for the future. They rightly demonstrate the methods that brought the congregation this far. We hope to gain more support by showing how valuable these methods are.

The first part of our story will detail the history leading up to the time when the precious black flock arrived at St. Mary's. Much of this early history was related by virtue of an historian, Father Cyprian Davis[3], O. S. B. (Order of Saint Benedict), well known for his scholarship and ability to portray, accurately, the life and times of black Catholics.

---

[3] The History of Black Catholics in the United States. Cyprian Davis, O.S.B. The Crossroad Publishing Company, 2002

CHAPTER ONE
Historical Antecedents to Sacred Heart

John Lynch

People who listen to us will not be able to understand much about what goes on within the walls of Sacred Heart without understanding something about the history of black Catholics and their relationship to the Church. The curious thing is that many people, both black and white, are often surprised to hear of black Catholics. For much of its history, Catholicism has been associated with white people. There are good reasons why this is so. But, we will point out immediately that black people have had a long and intense, but not always fruitful relationship with the Church.

Consider, for example, that the Old Testament refers to the land of Kush. We know that the reference usually meant what later became known as Nubia. In Isaiah 18:1-2, the passage describes Nubian warriors. They were from a black African nation that had its own pharaohs. In about the sixth century A.D., Justinian, emperor of the Roman Empire sent missionaries to Nubia. His missionaries supported the official teachings of the Catholic Church. Although there were competing Christian missionaries, a large portion of Nubia continued to profess a form of Catholicism. Ethiopia had become largely Christian two centuries before. In fact, Christianity flourished in Ethiopia before the Church was established in Ireland or England. Consequently, it is fair to say that black Africans were a fundamental part of early Christianity. This fact, like so many others that end up missing from the history of black Africans, alters the picture of black people. Christianity was not brought to Africa by slavers. Black Christians were there.[4]

The ungodly horror of slavery was the rock on which black Catholicism foundered.

The Corrupting Influence of Slavery

The Church has always been caught between the horns of a very difficult dilemma. In order to survive as an institution, it must support the needs of its parishes. When those parishes insist upon an ungodly path, the Church risks losing its membership if it insists that the congregation follow God's word and demonstrate moral behavior. The Church is further hampered by its reliance on fallible individuals. Its bishops and priests have to make the hard choices as representatives of the Church. If the cardinals and Popes do not compel proper choices, the result is a departure from the values on which the Church is founded. When the religious come down on the side of venal, corrupt or simply misguided parishioners, and the cardinals and Popes do not intervene, the results are ugly. Such was the case with regard to slavery and racism.

Because Sacred Heart has had its own history of conflict with bishops, cardinals and other religious around racial issues, we need to examine the broader history of the Church in this regard.

Again, we can thank Father Cyprian Davis[5] and his excellent work for the historical references in this chapter.

---

4   Ibid., pp. 2-13.

5   Ibid., pp. 20 - 66

Slavery, its Seductions and Justifications

In 1537, a Dominican Friar, Bartolome de Las Casas, documented the brutality and injustices inflicted on Indians in the Dominican Republic by the Spaniards. Pope Paul III issued a papal letter in which he detailed the rights of the Indians and the injustices of enslavement. The letter had no effect. The religious ministering to the Spanish in the Dominican Republic just ignored their Pope.

What was it about slavery that seduced religious institutions of all kinds to abandon their beliefs and support the degradation of human beings by human beings? The answer is simple.

Slavery was, and is, immensely profitable.

And yes, may God have mercy, slavery still exists.

Bishop John Carroll, the first bishop of the U.S. was a slave owner.

Jesuits, Vincentians, and other religious orders, both priests and nuns, owned slaves.

The denigration of black people under slavery cried out for a response from the Church. Having chosen to preserve itself by remaining silent in support of its white parishioners, the Church compounded the indignity by allowing its bishops to join in the abominations against black people. For example, St. Martin De Porres made his vows as a Dominican lay brother in spite of a decree from a Church Council that no African, Indian, mestizo or mulatto could be ordained as a priest or professed as a religious in any of the Spanish colonies. The justification for the decree is painfully revealing. The decree was issued so as to maintain respect for the priestly and religious offices and to maintain doctrinal purity. We have no doubt about whose respect was maintained by such a decree.

Reading between these lines offers an explanation for the behavior of the religious. With slavery so profitable, slave-owning Catholics had enormous influence with church leaders. Since the church leaders themselves were, at times, slave owners, there was no incentive to upset the trade. In fact, there was quite a lot of incentive to justify the trade so as to salve bruised and battered consciences.

A number of attempts were made by American bishops to defend slavery. To rationalize, they used biblical references and the writings of various theologians and philosophers.

Aristotle had said that some people were born to be enslaved and had to be ruled by force.

Priests said that slavery was justified because it led to the baptism and salvation of the slaves.

Priests also sought to justify slavery by suggesting that it was acceptable to enslave people who had been captured in a "just" war. The reality was that any war against those considered to be Muslim, meaning Africa, could be counted by the Spaniards as just.

None of these tortured justifications could stand up against the power of the Word. Those who truly adhered to the Word of God were, in every case, able to dismantle the arguments used to defend slavery. Those who knew the Word of God in their hearts were forced, by their consciences, to make a choice between godly words and ungodly deeds.

Courageous Church Leaders

There are instances of individual priests and bishops who made valiant attempts to counter the oppressive weight of public opinion in the US, the direct assaults by slavery profiteers and the justifications by Church hierarchy. These individuals made the personal choice to follow the Word, often at great expense to themselves.

In 1544, the friar, Bartolome de Las Casas, now a bishop in Chiapas Mexico, instructed his priests that they were not to give absolution to slaveholders until they promised to grant the slaves their freedom and reimbursed them for their labor. At Easter time in 1544, slaveholders rioted because they could not receive the sacraments. The bishop, in the face of violent opposition from both Catholic slaveholders and clergy, returned to Spain and resigned his see.

John England, the first bishop of Charleston, S.C., opened a school to teach the children of free black families. The white people raised such opposition that there was a riot. The bishop was forced to close the school.

There are several conclusions that we might draw from these descriptions:

The Church is dependent on its parishioners for its survival.

The Church is often put into the awkward position of choosing between its professed values and the things it feels compelled to do to survive as an institution.

The corrupting influences of wealth and power can be seen in any individual or institution that does not zealously guard against these seductions.

Those who allow themselves to be corrupted by the quest for wealth and power must dehumanize those who are their victims in order to protect their own self-esteem.

The Church, having fallible human beings as its representatives, is subject to the same error as other, non-religious human beings.

There are always, thank God, individuals who are ready to sacrifice themselves, their positions, their sustenance, even their physical well being to stand for the Word.

Those leaders who make such sacrifices have been a blessing from God to the oppressed of the earth.

The Church as a Beacon of Faith

While it is true that the record of the Church during the horror of slavery was not a stellar one, black people continued to find a light of hope in its message from God. The message is one that is particularly attractive to the poor and disenfranchised. Simply put, it is that everyone is equal in the sight of God. For black people, especially, this message provided a reason to hold on to their aspirations even

5

under the most brutal conditions. They looked to the Church to lead the fight against the continuing assault from white people on the most basic elements of humanity among black people. For a long time, black people waited in vain. But black people are patient and strong. Ultimately, their patience paid off. Ultimately, the Church could no longer ignore the difference between what it preached and what it practiced. The convergence of word and deed had first to chip away at the strong resistance of white people in the US. After decades more than two hundred years of democracy in the US, the struggle to overcome the deeply embedded antagonisms of white people toward black people continues.

Black people have often found sustenance and strength in collaboration and mutual support. In spite of its weak record in defense of black people, the Church provides numerous opportunities for collaboration. For this reason the Church draws many of the oppressed of the earth, including black people, to itself. As early as the 15th Century and continuing into the Spanish colonies, the Church used a kind of confraternity of lay people as a means to evangelize both slave and free black people, both male and female. These groups were devoted to mutual support. They bore names such as, "Most Holy Sacrament," "Our Lady of the Kings" and "Our Lady of the Rosary." They usually had a chapel where Mass was offered for the deceased. They celebrated the feasts of the Saints and provided charitable works for the benefit of both members and non-members. Because of the harsh attacks these innocent people had to endure, the confraternities often provided mutual security and protection along with professional aid. Clearly, all of these collaborative and mutually beneficial practices led to an increase in religious fervor, an outcome that strengthened devotion to the Church.

A strong case can be made for the fact that the present day group, The Knights of St. Peter Claver, is a close relative of the early confraternities. Once again, the very existence of the Knights provides testimony to the patience and tenacity of black people. The Knights were formed essentially because black people were not allowed to join The Knights of Columbus, an established confraternity for white people within the Church. Black people, once again, were forced to provide for themselves that which white people refused to share. The beauty of such an outcome is that, once again, black people had an opportunity to demonstrate their own power, resilience and self-reliance in the face of unremitting antagonism. The ugly side of the outcome is that, once again, white people failed to take advantage of an opportunity to get to know black people as capable human beings.

Whenever we make such a statement, we feel compelled to acknowledge our white brothers and sisters who share with us a basic humanity in spite of degrading cultural practices. Indeed, we are proud to show that the parishioners of Sacred Heart, as well as the Knights of St. Peter Claver, welcome human beings of every color.

> My grandparents house was at Farnsworth and Chene
> My wife and I have lived here all of our lives.
> We first came here in 1967 to the Guest House at the school.
> Recently we moved to South Lyons near Brighton
> "The Knights of Peter Claver must have been out of their minds because they asked a white, Polack, businessman to join."
> We stay because it's family.
> Our godchildren are here. They adopted us.
> We've been to churches across the world.
> When we moved to South Lyon, we asked Father Thomas to bless our house, which he did.
> We have extended the boundaries of Sacred Heart to South Lyon.
> There is a spirit here.
> People here have usually come from a Baptist background... they want to be preached to.
> I came out of churches where you were in and out in three raps.
>
> Joe Palkowski

Joe Palkowski's testimony confirms our observation that disenfranchised people of all types share a common burden and can find strength and support among those who struggle.

7

I was born in Racine, Wisconsin in 1938, the year St. Peter Claver parishioners became the new Sacred Heart parish. I was part of the Racine Dominican community from 1956 until 1971. In 1969, I was sent to teach at Nativity High School. When Judy Carty, at the time a sister from another community, came to Nativity looking for sisters to help her re-open the convent at Sacred Heart, I went with her to see if that convent would have a space where I could work at my sculpture. Even though there were not many parishioners, I felt immediately that I was home. The convent had plenty of space, including a fairly good-sized basement for me to work. I moved right away.

I remained in the convent until 1971. Many things had changed, both in the Church and in myself. I decided to leave my religious community.

The reason I have stayed here is that I have always felt Sacred Heart is as close as I have seen to what Jesus meant to do when He established His Church. Everyone here is like family. Even though I am white, they have accepted me and made me a part of them. When I am talking to anyone who is a member of Sacred Heart, I feel that we share some common values. We believe in justice for everyone, especially those who are less fortunate. We support political candidates and policies that ensure equitable treatment for everyone. We know that God is with us, to forgive, to direct, to save, and to support us in every action and in every suffering of our lives. We encourage, support and stand by each member of our parish family when they are in need. Our liturgy is a sincere expression of who we are, especially at the Kiss of Peace. And most of this spirit of unity is due to our wonderful pastor, Father Thomas.

Michaela Terrell

Michaela Terrell's testimony gives us specific detail about the values that hold people together at Sacred Heart. We can imagine that it was just such values that prompted black people in times past to view the Church as a lonely beacon of hope in a baffling and incredibly cruel environment.

8

War and the Church as Liberators

For all of those who paid attention in school, we know that the American Civil War did not start as a war to free the slaves. It was, instead, a war to preserve the union. When the unionists of the North realized that the bloody carnage would continue with no end in sight, the leaders decided to ennoble the mission with a declaration to end the "peculiar institution" of slavery. Not coincidentally, that also allowed them to enlist the aid of a sort of third column in the South, the slaves on Confederate plantations. Black people were given a chance to take up arms to fight for their freedom. To put that another way, war was the price of freedom.

There was another war that had essentially the same effect. In the early 1700's, the English and French had combined forces to drive the Spanish out. The Spanish had been developing Florida as a military outpost for almost 150 years to protect its holdings in the new world. Black people both slave and free, were a large part of the population around St. Augustine, the oldest home for black people in the US. The English settlements in the Carolinas and Georgia provided a base from which military expeditions could be carried out against the Spanish. To counter this threat, the Spanish invited the slaves in those territories to escape their masters and go to Florida where they would be given their freedom. The one condition was that they convert to Catholicism. In this case, not only war, but also Catholicism was the price for freedom.

We tread on dangerous ground when we describe another war about which black people do not like to talk. That is the war that is fought daily on the streets of Detroit, other major urban areas and in the public schools of these urban areas. This war of black people against black people has caused incredible attrition. Yet, because of the historical mistreatment of black people by white law enforcement, black people are reluctant to call for aid to reduce the carnage. The main point is that the Church, once again, has been the beneficiary of this war. Catholic schools in the US had, at one time, a jealously guarded reputation for academic excellence and, above all, strict discipline. Many black people, as well as white people, sought refuge for their children in Catholic schools to protect them from the ravages of the streets and public schools. The price for admission was often conversion to Catholicism. If not immediate conversion, then certainly exposure to religion classes, required attendance at Mass and other forms of overt and subtle proselytizing often led to eventual conversion. Once again, the price of freedom was Catholicism.

> We lived in the Brewster-Douglas projects about 1950.
> My brother and I were going to Bishop public school. I was in kindergarten and he was in first grade.
> He was beaten up going to and from school.
> My mother was Baptist from Georgia.
> Mom brought us to Sacred Heart to get away from the violence.
> My brother didn't get beaten up anymore.
>
> Karoy Brooks

Stories such as this one show that the Church and Sacred Heart offered refuge from the difficult circumstances in the poor communities under siege. To victims of the mean streets, the "price of freedom" was well worth paying. In fact, parents who sent their children to Sacred Heart under duress often found that they had secured an avenue to peace in a much broader sense than they had envisioned. The legacy of Sacred Heart includes a set of values that, if followed, leads to a personal peace that is extremely gratifying.

Before we continue our story, we need to bring to the forefront of our consciousness a reality that we do not often acknowledge openly. Any story of the journey of black people through the US could very well become a continuing and strident attack on white people. Black people do not need more than a moment's reflection to know that there has been any number of courageous white people who risked life and limb to protect black people from harm and to redress the effects of past harms.

The priests and nuns of the Catholic Church are, arguably, the best examples of such selfless people. Quakers are another recognizable group who are to be commended for their almost supernatural efforts to come to our aid. Without white people, there would have been no underground railroad.

We want to make this absolutely clear. This story is by no means an effort to refresh our memories of the horrors perpetrated against us so as to increase our desire for retribution. The glory of Catholic teachings is that such a path is destructive for everyone. We also would not want an outcome that has us distance ourselves from white people who are also human beings and children of God. That path leads to continued separation that, in turn, leads to misunderstanding, hatred and war. On the contrary, we want to say at the outset that we are profoundly grateful for the Church, especially its priests and nuns who, in spite of some exceptions, provided the support we desperately needed to begin to overcome the ongoing effects of the horror.

Trials and Tribulations of the Church Liberators

Priests and nuns, to serve the black community, often have to live in the same conditions, the same neighborhoods and face the same disdain that black people face. Most often, this means the religious have to experience the same effects of grinding poverty that black people have had to face for generations.

> Do you remember those little cardboard houses up and down the street?
> We used to play in what we called, "The alley." Remember that little place between the school and the playground...all dirt and cinders?
> The original school looked like a little old wooden schoolhouse.
>
> Leroy left because the nuns did not tolerate bad behavior.
> If you did something wrong, you were gone.
> There was no negotiating.
> They set the rules and you abided by them.
> No second or third chances.
> They set the rules when you walked in the door and that was it.
>
> Josephine Carter

The lighthearted description of "cardboard houses" gives us some indication of the kind of poverty affecting the neighborhood around

Sacred Heart, its rectory and its convent. Notice that there is no evident bitterness in the description of either the houses or the "alley." Those conditions were taken for granted. Josephine Carter's description confirms our conclusions both about the conditions under which the nuns and their charges lived as well as our convictions about the reasons the nuns were so effective. The nuns "did not tolerate bad behavior."

A newspaper article in The Detroit Times written in November of 1956 gives a much more graphic account of what the Felician nuns faced when they took on the assignment at Sacred Heart. Let us warn you. If this account does not break your heart, you don't have one.

Police to the Rescue
Nuns' Rundown Home Painted

Thirty-five policemen from Hunt Station today were painting the home of the Felician Sisters at 970 Eliot, because a veteran patrolman was softhearted and his inspector was suspicious.

The patrolman is Aldridge Baughman, 51, who is assigned to the Eastern Market beat near the Sisters' home. A month ago Inspector John Carnaghie learned that Baughman was systematically begging surplus produce from the wholesalers on his beat. Carnaghie, suspicious like any good policeman, wanted to know why. He assigned Lt. James Cole to trail Baughman.

35 Volunteers

Cole found each day Baughman was going from work to the Sisters' home with his leftovers and leaving it in their kitchen. Investigating, Cole found out why. The larder was pitifully vacant. One meal consisted entirely of sliced oranges. He found, too, that the home was sadly run down through no fault of the Sisters. It needed painting and the Sisters could not afford paint, let alone the painters.

A Jewish Shriner

As he called for volunteers, each platoon stepped forward as one man, chorusing: "When do we go to work?" The 35 all brought old clothes to the station house and were ready for action this morning. They were men of all faiths. Baughman, whose concern for the Sisters supplied the original spark, is of the Jewish faith and belongs to the Shriners.

Answer to Prayer

Beaming Sister Anthony, the Mother Superior, said: "This is the answer to our prayers to St. Anthony. What wonderful men these are."

Meanwhile, the food problem has been solved for the Sisters. Members of the Eastern Market Association have agreed each day to donate certain excess commodities so there will be no more bare cupboards.

Rely on donations

The LKA Paint Co. learned of the program and contributed the paint. The nuns, members of the Felician Order, teach at a school next door for children who are on the borderline of becoming delinquents, largely because of unfortunate home conditions. Their financial plight, Cole said, is because the Sisters are forced to rely almost entirely on contributions.

Sacred Heart Archives

Except for the blatant misrepresentation about "the children who are on the borderline of becoming delinqluents..." the article gives a clear picture of the conditions under which this noble order of nuns had to live to carry out their mission in aid of black people.

The following was excerpted from a letter from the Holy Ghost Fathers at Sacred Heart to Detroit Catholics asking for contributions. It gives further evidence of the conditions faced by both priests and nuns.

Dear Friend,

There are those who find it difficult to believe that, in these days of widespread employment and high wages, there are priests and nuns who must work in this prosperous city for nothing more than their room and board. Such, however, is the case here, because the regular income of the parish makes it impossible to do otherwise. Of the five priests here, one receives no salary at all and the combined salaries of the other four amount to $80 per month per man. The chaplainry of Harper Hospital, entrusted to us by His Eminence, the Cardinal, is a work of mercy and charity and has no salary attached to it.

As for the good Sisters of the Felician Order who work so hard and unselfishly in our school, only four of the thirteen receive

13

any salary whatsoever, and what these four receive is but a mere pittance when one considers the amount of work they do and the good they accomplish. Were we obliged to pay each Sister the miserably poor salary to which she is entitled (about $2.00 per day) and were they unwilling to sacrifice themselves without hope of financial return, we would be forced to close our school and thus deprive over four hundred children of the priceless training provided by the Sisters – the only training that many of them receive, but which they need badly.

Sacred Heart Archives

The Rev. Henry J. Montambeau, C. S. Sp., Pastor, and the four parish priests signed this letter. The letter goes on to describe the deplorable state of both the rectory and the convent.

Clearly, these two orders of religious, Felician nuns and Holy Ghost priests lived the life that Christ demonstrated.

The Catholic Church is unique in its ability to prepare its religious for this difficult duty on the front lines of racism in the U.S. The vows of poverty, chastity and obedience that many religious take, along with an abiding faith in God, are the bare minimum armor required to face what reluctant black families have had to face for centuries to sustain life and soul against incredible odds.

The Parish

We want to give you a sense of what "parish" means so that you will understand some of the dynamics in the life of a Catholic congregation in the middle part of the twentieth century. The local parish is the instrument through which the Church transmits God's truths and influences the lives of its congregants. In the words of Pope John Paul II, the parish is "The Church placed in the neighborhoods of humanity." He goes on to say, "it is one of the major assets of Christianity, and for the vast majority of the faithful it remains the focal point for the ordinary practice of the faith." This statement came from *Christifidelis Laici,*[6] Post Synodal Apostolic

---

[6] http://www.vatican.va/holy_father_/john_paul_ii/apost_exhortation/documents/hf_jp_ii_exh_30121988_christifidelis_laici_en.html

Exhortation. The statement is important to us because it puts the Church on record as dependent on the parish to carry out its mission in the service of God.

To repeat, the parish is in the neighborhood. It is the focal point for the ordinary practice of the faith. The consequences are obvious. The pastor is the principle source of guidance and the most conspicuous representative of the Church. As a matter of practical reality, the pastor is the one member of the Church hierarchy that most Catholics are likely to see in person. What he does with the congregation is likely to define for them what they can expect from the Church. In military language, the pastor is the battlefield lieutenant. He leads the charge in conducting the mission of the Church. The area of operation is the neighborhood.

When immigrants arrive in the US, they are likely to head for the neighborhood where people like themselves have already settled. Detroit history, like that of any other major urban area of the US, is a history of immigrant groups. We can imagine the arrivals in a state of mild shock. This would be true whether they came in the hope of improving their fortunes or out of desperation to leave an awful situation. In a completely strange environment, they would appreciate having a safe place to congregate with people like themselves, people who spoke their language and shared the same cultural traditions. That place was likely to be the parish church. The result is that the history of parishes in Detroit parallels the history of immigrant arrivals.

Rarely was a church built or a parish begun to serve a combination of ethnic groups. Each parish church was likely to have been built by a particular ethnic group to serve its own needs. St. Anne was French, given its early history in Detroit at Fort Pontchartrain. It is the oldest continuously active parish in the northern US. Our Lady of Sorrows was built by and for the Belgians. St. Charles was intended to be Belgian, but Detroit was becoming more cosmopolitan at the time, 1886. Belgians were predominant, but there were also French, German, Polish and English-speaking congregants. St. Peter was established for Lithuanians. Holy Cross was Hungarian. Our Lady of Mt. Carmel served Polish immigrants. Sacred Heart was designed by Germans for Germans. The list could go on.

Leslie Tentler[7], renowned historian, tells about the increase in Detroit's population between 1920 and 1925. Many of the immigrants included Catholic groups that had not been represented earlier. To accommodate this influx, Bishop Gallagher established thirty-eight foreign language parishes, each devoted to a particular group. Among these were Russian, Maltese, Mexican, Croatian and Slovenian. During this period, he also authorized a second parish for Detroit's black Catholics. The point we would like to make is that one could easily attribute this ethnic exclusivity to racism if the original intent is not taken into consideration.

This typical scenario of how parishes came to be founded does not support, on its face, the charge of racism in the Church. It reflects, instead, the means by which the Church survives. The parish gives its congregation the support it needs and, in return, the congregation supports the church. All of the groups we have named came as strangers to a strange land. The parish was often the only place where they could find people like themselves who would understand their fears and nurture their aspirations.

In a refrain to which we will return in one way or another, we know that black people, in spite of being in America as one of its oldest ethnic groups from foreign soil, remain "strangers in a strange land." The earlier ethnic groups were of European stock. They assimilated each other as they found common ground in advancing their interests. The history of Detroit and the history of the parish reflect the history of the US. The disheartening truth is that black people have been faced with innumerable obstacles and persistent difficulty in assimilating. These continue to this very day.

---

[7]   Seasons of Grace: A History of the Catholic Archdiocese of Detroit.
      Leslie Woodcock Tentler. Great Lakes Book Series, 1990, pp. 306 – 307.
      We are grateful to Jamil Allah for introducing us to this excellent work.

When Neighborhoods Change

Cultural clashes often occurred when one ethnic group replaced another in a particular parish. The replacement happened because the neighborhood around the parish changed. The immigrants who founded the parish usually became more affluent. The old houses that they occupied no longer suited their needs. They looked for more comfortable surroundings. As the first few left, other immigrants of lesser means found the old homes perfect for their meager resources. The new arrivals told their relatives and friends about the great houses they found. In due course, the change in the neighborhood accelerated. It became more pronounced and obvious that a new group was replacing the old. It happened when the Germans replaced the French, when the Italians replaced the Germans and so on.

We can give a, perhaps, fictional example. The parish church that was once a place where the Germans could relax among familiar faces, accents and traditions becomes an uncomfortable place when Italians arrive who might be considered odd by the Germans. This occurs because the Italians are not likely to know the German rules of decorum and behave in ways which could seem outlandish to the Germans. The Italians are made uncomfortable by the obvious disdain they see on the faces and in the reactions of the Germans. These reactions could be very similar when the Belgians replace the Italians and when the Lithuanians replace the Belgians.

In effect, this fictional account would not change regardless of the ethnic groups under consideration. The pattern is likely to repeat itself whether we are talking about race, color, creed, social status or any other line of demarcation in an increasingly fractured society. Sacred Heart also experienced this phenomenon.

Aug. 7, 1938

Rt. Rev. Archbishop Edward Mooney,

Will you please reconsider the change in Sacred Heart Church, Rivard and Eliot Streets? We have been Parishioners in this Church for over forty years and have known Rev. Hubert Klenner for fifteen years or more.

After building up the Parish to what it is now and then seeing the Negroes come in and knock it down is more than we can stand.

Why not see our point of view? We have attended Sacred Heart church ever since we were able to walk. It feels strange to attend any other Church than Sacred Heart Church on Sundays; and we dislike stepping out after these long years. Why not let the Negroes stay at St. Peter Claver Church and let Rev. Hubert Klenner reign as Pastor as long as he lives.

Cordially Yours,
The Parishioners of Sacred Heart Church

Sacred Heart Archives

The sentiments expressed in the letter concerning black people are a reflection of the prevailing attitudes of the time and, perhaps, continuing to this day. However, let us not forget the point. Evidence of racism in this letter notwithstanding, the attempt to prevent another culture from taking over Sacred Heart has a clear precedent. The following passage was excerpted from a long letter describing the history of Sacred Heart. The purpose was to convince Bishop Gallagher to allow the Germans to keep the church rather than give it to the Italians. Since this happened prior to the arrival of the African Americans, we can see that racism, if any, is not the central issue.

...the list of parishioners (at Sacred Heart) suffered a gradual and steady decline so that in some quarters it was considered advisable to turn it over to the Italian Catholics. However, the German residents of the parish considered themselves still capable of maintaining the parish and under date of March 20, 1922, laid their cause before the Rt. Rev. Bishop James Gallagher, D.D. and, to their joy and great satisfaction, with favorable results.

Sacred Heart Archives

This letter did not contain any disparaging remarks from the Germans about the Italians, but the intent to prevent the Italians from using the church along with the Germans, or in place of them, was still the same.

When a change in a parish occurs, the pastor responds in whatever way is characteristic for him. Sometimes his diplomatic skills are up to the task of helping to make a smooth transition. In too many cases, he has become co-opted by the founding congregation. Often, he is of the same ethnic or social group as the founders. He identifies with them and, consciously or unconsciously, shows bias in support of those whom he has come to love and trust and against those who would displace them.

When the pastor and the congregation agree that the usurpers are wronging them, they appeal to the bishop. Not even Solomon could make a decision that would satisfy both Germans and Italians. The result is that the pastor and his flock leave and the Italians have a new church of German design. Outcomes such as this would remain the same regardless of what ethnic group replaced the resident one.

Black Migration

When black people enter a neighborhood, the virulence of the reactions to their presence reaches an intensity amazing to behold. The stakes go up in at least two senses of the term, physical and monetary. Defenses go up also, such as anger, attacks, riots and, sooner or later, flight. When black people move in, flight takes place sooner more often than later.

These neighborhood effects were certainly evident and very pronounced around the turn of the century when black people arrived in Detroit in great numbers. We do not have to recount all that transpired in the South to know that black people, given a modicum of opportunity, would literally shake the dust of the South from their feet to take advantage of the slightest promise of a better life.

The opportunities provided by the auto industry were glorious beyond the wildest dreams of a strong black person gazing into a starry night on a hardscrabble farm. Factory wages and benefits represented the "promised land" compared to the uncertain and desperate life of a sharecropper in the South.

The migration began.

Understand that we are not talking about immigrants from foreign lands now. We are talking about internal migration, from one area of the US to another.

Black people carry their status in their faces.

There is nowhere to hide.
There is no way to assimilate.
There is no way to negotiate.
Only the strong survive.
Black people are strong.

John Lynch

But even black people...patient, strong, loving, kind, God-fearing black people can take just so much. The inevitable happens.

The Detroit Race Riots of 1943

The origins of Sacred Heart in the basement of a school were set in a time of intense stress stemming from painful conditions in the surrounding black communities. These conditions form a litany of horrors. All of the historical preconditions seemed to accumulate in concentrated form in the American urban ghettoes.

The influx of black people from the South to take manufacturing jobs led to a shortage of housing, transportation, education and recreation.

The arriving immigrants faced bigotry that was as pervasive and virulent as any in the South.

There were long lines everywhere.

Black people were excluded from all public housing except the Brewster projects. For this reason, the Brewster projects became an oasis in the middle of the turmoil. The projects housed a variety of black people from all economic levels.

Many black people, who were not fortunate enough to live in housing such as the Brewster projects, lived in housing without indoor plumbing, but paid rent two to three times higher than white people with similar amenities.

Black people suffered from a segregated military, discrimination in public accommodations and mistreatment by the police.

Whites formed neighborhood groups to keep black people out.

White vigilantes would perpetrate acts of violence against any black person unlucky enough to be in the wrong place at the wrong time.

Black people had to put extraordinary effort into securing housing in the Sojourner Truth projects.

The result of all of these indignities was that the black population, finally fed up, engaged in 36 hours of rioting in 1943.[8]

Thirty-six lives were lost, of which 25 were black.

More than 1800 were arrested for looting and other incidents.

Black people were the vast majority of those arrested.

The police killed only black people...17 of them.

This graphic picture gives us some insight into the challenges facing black people in Detroit about the time period of interest to us.

---

[8]   1943 Riots. http://libarts.udmercy.edu/paradisevalley/home.htm

CHAPTER TWO
The Early Years
1930's to 1950's

John Lynch

We would do well to describe the neighborhood and general conditions in which our little congregation started out. In the years prior to the 1943 riots in Detroit, black people were under siege. Life was incredibly difficult as you might well imagine from the description of those riots. In the US, lynching occurred at the rate of about one each day. Over a 10-year period, 3,000 black people died at the hands of white mobs. Black people were segregated into ghettoes apart from whites. Jobs were usually unavailable to black people and agriculture was one of the few means of survival. Black people were a feared and despised minority subject to various forms of often-gratuitous mistreatment.

After the turn of the century, Detroit's black population grew rapidly as Southerners migrated north to escape the poverty associated with sharecropping and to seek better-paying factory jobs. The migrants settled in an area on the east side that came to be known as "Black Bottom." The term used did not originally refer to the presence of black people. Instead, as the migrants were former agrarians, the term referred to the rich black soil that characterized the area before development. Hastings Street was the main thoroughfare.

Paradise Valley

Hastings Street was the center of African American culture from the early 1930's to the 1960's. Even prior to that time, the black culture was thriving. In a Detroit News article by Vivian Baulch[9] called "Paradise Valley and Black Bottom," she reports much of the following.

Around 1910, Detroit had a black population of about 6,000 and owned a couple of dozen businesses. With the auto industry attracting large numbers, by 1920 Detroit's African-Americans had 350 businesses. These included a movie theater, a pawn shop, a co-op grocery and a bank. Numerous other businesses and professionals included physicians, lawyers, barbers, dentists, cartage companies, tailors,

---

[9]   Paradise Valley. Vivian Baulch. http://info.detnews.com/history/index. cfm?id=174&category=life

restaurants, real estate dealers, druggists, undertakers, employment agencies and, to top it off, a candy maker.

Sacred Heart was at the epicenter of the action since this area of vitality was centered on the near east side of downtown Detroit. The important streets were St. Antoine, Hastings, Brush, John R., Gratiot, Vernor, Madison, Beacon, Elmwood, Larned and Lafayette.

The name, "Paradise Valley," probably came from the prevalence of the "Paradise" tree that was a common sight in the rich bottomlands of which the area was composed. The name turned out to be apt even though the community struggled against vicious racism and general poverty. The ever-adaptable black population developed a unique culture which contributed to their survival under difficult circumstances. To escape sometimes horrifying realities, Detroit's black people took solace in highly popular clubs such as, Club Three Sixes, El Sino, Pendennies, 606 Horse Shoe, B&C Club, Congo Lounge, Gay 90's Club, Royal Blue Bar, and the Bluebird Inn.

The rigidly segregated boundaries of the area had the ironic effect of solidifying the community and, thereby, increasing its self-identity and corresponding strength and resourcefulness. The name "Paradise Valley" became synonymous with a richly effervescent culture that came to recognize its own distinct contribution to the city of Detroit. That recognition of itself was affirmed by the general acknowledgement of the informal mayor, Roy Lightfoot. Much of the strength of the community rested in the hopes black people had in their heroes such as Jesse Owens, the Olympic star who caused Adolph Hitler such pain. His visit to the Valley inspired a celebration. Another world famous hero was, of course, the Brown Bomber, Joe Louis, who was the Valley's favorite son. His mother, Lily Brooks, lived on McDougall.

Famous people, people who had left the degradation behind, were often cited as an inspiration in keeping hope alive in the tough times. Listen to the voices of Sacred Heart.

I have been Catholic all of my life.
My grandfather was a slave in Virginia and fought in the Civil War.
He became Catholic as a slave.
He was baptized and married in the Church.
I was born in 1916 and baptized at St. Peter Claver. My aunt was housekeeper there.
My brothers were altar boys.
Father Thiefels gave my daughter her paint set.
Priests would go to St. Peter Claver as part of their training as missionaries.
The first black priest, Father Dukette, was ordained at the cathedral.
I was there.
Steppin' Fetchit would attend Saint Peter Claver at Easter time.
A number of famous people would attend, including the attorney who worked with Clarence Darrow.

Ada Maxwell

People do not realize that Detroit is the source of some of the greatest jazz musicians as well as other notables. Paul Chambers, bassist, and Louis Hayes, drummer, lived in my neighborhood. Yussef Lateef used to play at Klines' Show Bar.

Great athletes of historical importance grew up in the neighborhood.
Jesse Owens lived across the street from me on Inverness.
Joe Louis worked out at Brewster Center.

My cousin, Donald Goines, wrote a novel, "Never Die Alone," which has now been made into a movie.

I have been a jazz enthusiast all of my life. I am known for my collection of music, especially at Baker's Keyboard Lounge, the oldest jazz club in continuous operation in the U.S. At Baker's, they call me "Dr. Boo Boo."

Scott Bradford

As Ada Maxwell and Scott Bradford would attest, we recall fondly the glories of the time, but the conditions under which black people had to live were appalling.

The Public Broadcasting System (PBS) produced a documentary that described the situation leading up to the 1943 race riots.[10] In that description we learn that in the years preceding the Second World War, Detroit had been torn apart by racial conflict. The Ku Klux Klan, an organization notorious for its violence against black people in support of its views of white supremacy, had found a welcoming home in Michigan. Black people had found jobs, but there was precious little housing for them. Black people were under siege by white people who not only guarded their neighborhoods against black encroachment, but also attacked those black people who purposely or inadvertently entered their areas. With both legal and de facto segregation, Detroit's 200,000 black people were ghettoized into sixty square blocks on the East Side. As a direct result, the sanitary conditions were outrageous. But in their indomitable spirit of survival, black people found a way to appropriate the name "Paradise Valley" to their own ends.

Here we get some semblance of the reality facing black people. The fact that we not only endured these indignities, but prospered is a tribute to our resourcefulness. That we found a way to enjoy life, using our own God-given talents, has to be a tribute to God's providence as He helped us to retain our integrity, our sanity and our faith. As a result, the name, "Paradise Valley," now connotes a vibrant and enriching black culture and not "deplorable sanitary conditions."

Eleanor Roosevelt

From an account offered by PBS[11] we also get a glimpse of the very welcome impact on the state of black people at the time by Eleanor Roosevelt, First Lady of the nation, and wife of Franklin Delano Roosevelt. Mrs. Roosevelt was known for her efforts on behalf of black people and other oppressed minorities. Her efforts were so visible that there were those who blamed her for the riots of 1943.

---

[10]   Riots 1943. http://www.pbs.org/wgbh/amex/eleanor/peopleevents/pande10.html

[11]   Eleanor Roosevelt. http://www.pbs.org/wgbh/amex/eleanor/index.html

According to the PBS account, the editors of the Mississippi *Jackson Daily News* sought to explain the causes of the riot. In a tone reflecting the fanaticism of the time, they blamed Eleanor Roosevelt's efforts on behalf of racial equality. They told of how black people attempted to put Mrs. Roosevelt's views into practice. The paper decried these attempts as evidence of the growing impudence and insolence of the Negro population.

From the vantage point of history, we can now appreciate what the phrase "growing impudence and insolence of the Negro population" meant to white people. It fully captures the thinking of the lords of the universe, the white people who had, until Paradise Valley, proved their supremacy to themselves by committing atrocities against black people. Now, white people would have to contend with a powerful people whose patience was exhausted.

But, black people have always had a number of champions like Eleanor Roosevelt. As in the Underground Railroad, there were people who were anguished at the despicable way black people were treated. The unwavering and active support for the cause of black people by influential white people such as Eleanor Roosevelt surely helped us in the years during which the Sacred Heart congregation developed. But, just as we must with any other human being, we must look at all of her pronouncements to determine the things with which we agree and those with which prudent people can reasonably disagree. Soon after the attack on Pearl Harbor, Mrs. Roosevelt said that things would improve "if we were all drafted and told what to do. Only then could we get the maximum service out of our citizens inasmuch as a higher authority would be there to tell us where we can be most useful and where our work is needed."

We do not want to be picky, but that sounds like the first step on a slippery slope toward totalitarianism and a sooner rather than later return to slavery. The point we wish to make is that even when black people accepted, gratefully, the support of well-meaning others, we needed to be on guard against unreflective support for those who expressed good will. That was a dangerous time indeed. We might add that the danger has not appreciably decreased. The price of freedom is eternal vigilance.

Black Catholics were counted among the perennial strangers in a strange land who used their ingenuity and mutual support as well as the support of people like Eleanor Roosevelt to thrive even while under continuing assault. Their faith bound them together and gave them a reason to seek each other out. The persistence of black people in attaching themselves to the Church was rewarded when some members of the Church hierarchy assumed the role of champion and recognized their duty to provide support to these true Catholics.

Origins at St. Mary

Among the parishes in the area, the one on which we focus was near Hastings Street. St. Mary, at the corner of St. Antoine and Monroe in what is now known as Greektown, was founded in 1835. The church was built for the Germans who were then a minority in a town of French people. After a series of religious orders administered the church, the Holy Ghost fathers took responsibility in 1893. They began establishing a ministry that embraced both African Americans and Mexicans.

The 1869 Catholic Directory list of Detroit diocesan churches includes a "chapel for colored people" tended by a Belgian priest. The reference does not mention where the chapel was located and the reference disappears after the 1873 edition. "Make Straight the Path," found in Sacred Heart's archives, describes what happens next.

> "The St. Mary's Poor and Orphan Society, initially a parish organization, was incorporated into the Detroit chapter of the St. Vincent de Paul Society in 1911, which greatly expanded its ability to provide assistance to the needy. The Society's most ambitious project, however, was to formally unite the city's African American Catholics into a single worship community that met in the basement of the St. Mary Parish school for its first service in 1911."
>
> Sacred Heart Archives

Again, we point out that there are numerous white people, guided by faith and love, who recognize a need among fellow human beings and meet the need at some sacrifice to themselves. St. Mary's Poor and Orphan Society is a good example. We also remind all those who hold opposite views that the black population was not, even under the appalling conditions of the time, suffused with hatred, but welcomed collaboration when it was offered in love and respect. The fact that Sacred Heart remains essentially a church of African Americans is an issue to which we will return.

Holy Ghost Priests

The Holy Ghost priests deserve a great deal of both praise and gratitude from African Americans. In fact, there is no way to tell the story of Sacred Heart without describing the mission of the priests and nuns who fought so valiantly on its behalf. The religious orders, Holy Ghost priests and Felician nuns figure prominently in our story because of their remarkable contributions to its congregation. Diocesan priests, such as Father Norman Thomas have, individually, contributed amazing feats to help Sacred Heart on its way. First, we will take a look at the origins of the Holy Ghost priests as a way of understanding how they came to be so important to us. We treat them first because it was they who were responsible for ministering to the early congregation.

We continue to rely on Father Cyprian Davis[12] and his definitive work in gathering the information that follows.

At about the same time that the black congregation began to meet in the basement of St Mary in 1911, the Roman Curia was intensely involved in examining the state of black Catholics in America. What they found was disconcerting at best. Even the most pious priests in America were so afraid of the reaction of their white congregations that they made no effort to help black people. Some priests were often so prejudiced themselves that in response to requests for aid, they would say, "They do not belong to my flock. They are not my concern." We are reminded of St. Peter's repeated response to the Roman soldiers and other challengers, "I know not the man." Still

_____

[12]   Op. Cit. pp. 196 - 207

some other priests and prelates were so convinced of the inferiority of black people that they counseled that black people should not aspire to higher status and civic equality, but to remain in a lowly condition. The Curia also found that there were proportionately few black Catholics compared to the total population of blacks. As late as the Detroit of 1938, Father Henry Thiefels reported that there were 140,000 Negroes. Of these, only 2500 were Catholic. These sorry numbers were the outcome of two prominent factors. There was little enthusiasm among the religious for ministry to black people and the white population despised and even attacked those who did minister to them.

The Curia decided that this sad state of affairs could be remedied only by religious who were both competent and dedicated to the work of ministry among black people. One of the three or four religious orders that met the criteria was the Congregation of the Holy Ghost.

The Congregation of the Holy Ghost (C. S. Sp.) had extensive experience in ministering to black people. They had been formed in 1848 from a combination of two missionary societies, the other being the Missionaries of the Immaculate Heart of Mary. One of the most heartening aspects of their approach to their work was that they, as a group, did not think of black people as inferior, but respected them and believed them to be deserving of equality. Please note that we have specified, "As a group." There is some evidence from the voices of the congregation that there were those, even among this stellar group of religious, who demonstrated a definite lack of fervor and, perhaps, some animosity in working with us.

> We moved to the Brewster projects in the 1940's and Sacred Heart Church was close.
> I was raised by my sister who was Catholic and so I was raised Catholic.
> When I came to Sacred Heart I was married to Thomas Butler.
> Father Murphy was Pastor. He was not fond of black people.
> He was pastor about 2 years after I came to Sacred Heart.
> Father Stegman became pastor. He didn't seem to understand

black people and didn't want to be bothered by black people.
Alma Swain

I remember that Father Stegman was the one who tried to get rid of this church. The black people were just coming in and he tried to stop it. He told us that there was a train going to come through and how would we like to hear that when there was a service.
A lot of black people did not stay in the church because of the priests.
A lot of them are prejudiced. They will take your money and not tell you what they are doing with it.
Lillie Brown

I remember Father Montambeau and Father Stegman.
My personal memory of Stegman is not bad. What I heard was from my folks.
They didn't think he was sympathetic toward the black community.
There were nuns here who felt like it was a punishment to be here at Sacred Heart.
I remember Sisters Mansueta, Stanislas and Ralph. Sister Mary Rosalima was the best teacher I have had.
I had a wonderful time here although there were some bad nuns (Sr. Ralph).
Pat Abner

But, black people had, by this time, become accustomed to taking the bitter with the sweet. They were still quite dependent on the help of good people. How the enlightened and godly members of the Holy Ghost priests came to the aid of black people is a story worth repeating.

The 300 hundred-year history of the Holy Ghost priests begins with Paul Francis Poullart des Places who was the son of an affluent lawyer and businessman in Paris, France. Instead of following his father's footsteps to the halls of parliament and French upper class life, he developed a relationship with the homeless and poor chimney sweeps of Paris. It was he who founded the earlier order in 1704 with the purpose of responding to both the material and spiritual needs of his fellow students in the seminary, many of whom were impoverished. The Seminary of the Holy Ghost assisted students so that they, in turn might aid the poor in rural France and overseas missions. These Holy Ghost priests, who now call themselves Spiritans, began missionary work in Africa in about 1800 and eventually became a presence in all of Sub-Saharan Africa.

Another person is given credit as the second founder of the order. Francis Mary Paul Libermann, born into a rabbinical Jewish family, converted to Catholicism while studying to become a rabbi. He has been called "The Incredible Jew." Of his conversion he said, "I have built myself a religion based on my reason and I see nothing wrong in following it, provided I do no harm to any of my fellow men." He initially founded the Congregation of the Holy Heart of Mary. With Papal encouragement, he was ordained as a priest explicitly for work in missions to black people, slaves and former slaves in French colonies of the Caribbean, the Indian Ocean and Africa.

This focus on overseas missions brought the priests to the attention of the Archconfratemity of Our Lady of Victories that, in 1839, had recommended the evangelization of the colored race. In 1848, Father Libermann's society was fused with the Holy Ghost priests of Father des Places and the combined order continued its missionary work.

This brief history of the origins of the Spiritans, the Holy Ghost Fathers, reveals a picture that affected us deeply.

Both Father des Places and Father Libermann were born to comfortable circumstances. Both could have gone along with their privileges to live lives of ease while enjoying the respect and even praise of others. However, both chose to devote their lives to the poor and disfranchised who are the despised of the earth. Father Libermann lets us know that his "reason" led him to his choice. Such reasoning had to be powerfully compelling for a person of Jewish origins to choose Catholicism over Judaism.

Both of these founders as well as their priests, from that time to now, paid extremely high prices for their commitments. In the poverty stricken environments in which they chose to work, they could expect, at the very least, ill health.

Often, they paid with their lives.

We should not be surprised, then, that in the America of 1911, in the Detroit of violent conflicts, when the bishop needed courageous, selfless, hard working priests who were comfortable living with people of color in dangerous conditions, he received a positive, even eager response from the Spiritans.

Diocesan Priests

Diocesan priests differ from priests who belong to a religious order only in the matter of hierarchy. A priest who belongs to a religious order is subject to the rules of that order and has pledged himself to advance the aims of that order. In the case of the Holy Ghost priests, now the Spiritans, they dedicate themselves to work among the poor and downtrodden of the earth. When such a priest is invited by the bishop to work in a diocese, he is subject also to the rules established by the bishop for that diocese. Consequently, the priest must account for his actions to both the Superior of the order and to the bishop.

A diocesan priest, such as Father Norman Thomas, is subject only to the bishop who has appointed him to the parish or to other work in the diocese. Sacred Heart has enjoyed the services of both diocesan and order priests. We make this point because the distinction has played an important role in the life of Sacred Heart.

Felician Sisters

The courage and resourcefulness of the male religious were matched and, arguably, exceeded by the female religious. We are quite conscious of the difficulty women have had, and still have, in a male-oriented world. The willingness of some women to go alone into places of danger without male protection is worthy of serious reflection. Nuns who dedicate themselves to a life of service to the poor and disfranchised are awe-inspiring.

The decision to embark on such a life is one not to be taken lightly. In their constitution, which can be found on the Felician web site, the Felician Sisters express the heart of the community's identity. That identity is based in a "call to service, service motivated by love of God, service to gain souls for Christ through a total self-giving in corporal and spiritual works of mercy." The first sisters in the community "were imbued with the conviction that they were to have a specific manner of performing works of mercy, namely, through inculcating true piety in all classes of society." The piety referred to was not one of pious practices, but a relationship with God known, loved and served. The Felician sisters take vows of poverty, chastity and obedience.

Let us reflect on what it would mean to African Americans in the Detroit of the 1920's and 1930's to work with a group of women who "performed works of mercy through total self-giving." White people, taken as a whole, seemed to be dedicated to the abuse and destruction of black people. Here were white women who gave themselves totally in service to God with the express purpose of aiding black people in dire need. We thank God for such people.

A person would not make such a commitment without serious and extensive preparation. The woman who would be a nun must pass through a series of steps, including both study and practice before she takes perpetual vows. These steps are similar to those through which a priest must pass.

During "Affiliation," a woman continues her life, but maintains contact with a Felician sister and shares in the community activities.

Upon entering the "Postulancy," the woman resides in the community and takes part in the daily life of the nuns.

During the "Novitiate," the woman studies the vows, rules and constitution. She also engages in some apostolic experience.

In a six-year period of "Temporary Profession of Vows," the woman can get the full meaning of living life as a nun.

The ultimate step is to take the "Perpetual Profession of Vows" in which the woman freely chooses to live in the Felician Community.[13]

---

[13]   http://www.sistersofst_felixof.htm

These rigorous and difficult steps help to make sure that the woman who becomes a nun knows what she is getting into and has every opportunity to review her decision before she takes her final vows. More than that, the Felician nun knows what the sisters are expected to do with their lives, that is, serve others who often are unable to help themselves.

The nuns and priests who worked with African Americans during the critical early stages of the growth of the congregation were serious and dedicated professionals. They came with the confidence and discipline that can only be developed over long periods of intense study and practice. We remain grateful for their dedication and sacrifice.

Just as it is difficult to fathom how other human beings can be so relentlessly antagonistic toward black people, we could find it equally difficult to appreciate what sacrifice it must have taken for white priests and nuns to live among us in spite of the derision, both expressed and implied, they must have endured from some of the people who looked like them. From the present vantage point of even partial privilege, those who did not experience the viciousness of that period probably have little idea of what their progenitors had to do to survive. In this relatively short historical period, black people have not only endured, but also prospered. So much so that recent generations of black children express little interest and even less appreciation for the road their ancestors had to travel. So be it. Perhaps it is better so. The hopeful outcome is that black people can more easily shed the self-destructive bitterness that could have accompanied a full appreciation of the horror. But, to gain some empathy for that road, let us try to imagine what lay ahead of the little congregation who found safety in the basement of a school.

Here they were, in an inhospitable and strange land, beset on all sides by unimaginably brutal forces. They had only their abiding faith in the providence of God to sustain them. They had chosen a Church that said all of the right words. They had encountered individual religious from that Church who were brave and self-sacrificing. This little band of brothers and sisters settled in to do what they knew how to do...pray.

The group of faithful black Catholics who met in the basement of a school would have had no way of knowing the distinguished legacy that they were initiating. What we all know is that when people allow themselves to be guided by God's Word, miracles happen... not necessarily the ones for which we pray, but ones which offer the best alternative to carry out God's plan.

In the following pages, our attempt will be to try to understand and explain how the Sacred Heart congregation, with its origins in the basement of Old St. Mary's school, came to be such a powerful influence in the life of its members and in the soul of an historic city as a result of devoting itself to living life as Jesus demonstrated. We admit that this is a tall order. If we are successful, we will be grateful, once again, to God and His mercy.

CHAPTER THREE
From St. Peter Claver to Sacred Heart

September 1, 1911
Old St. Mary's School
Beginning of St. Peter Claver
1914 November
Happy Thanksgiving!
A new worship site
is purchased,
and the first
Mass is
celebrated.
September 1, 1938
Great celebration — March from Eliot
and Beaubien to our new and current home,
SACRED HEART

Michaela Terrell

On the occasion of the Centennial Celebration of Sacred Heart, 1875 – 1975, a brief history was written. Statements from that history confirm our belief that a deep and abiding faith held black people together and enabled our people to do remarkable things.

It was not only because other parishes did not welcome black Catholics into their prejudiced congregations, but mostly because we wished to express our cultural experiences in religious life, that we organized our parish in 1911. Pride in a long cultural-religious history, more and more dominates the churches of black people. Thus, on September 1, 1911, Father Joseph Wuest, C. S. Sp., pastor of Old St. Mary's, met with eighteen persons who decided to establish a parish. A large classroom at St. Mary's School was made available and for three years served as a chapel for black Catholics in the city.

In 1914, our growing congregation purchased a small Episcopal Church located on Beaubien and Eliot streets. On Thanksgiving Day, Bishop John Foley dedicated the new church. The tireless efforts of a faith-filled people were rewarded with a new parish named St. Peter Claver.

We draw your attention to a part of the statement, "...other parishes did not welcome black Catholics into their prejudiced congregations..."

When I first came to Sacred Heart in the first grade, it was because black children were not allowed to go to Holy Rosary. Holy Rosary was within walking distance and I had to take a bus to get to Sacred Heart.

Rosemarie Block Evans

We lived in Conant Gardens. There were no black churches in our community. White churches would not accept blacks. No parochial schools would accept blacks. We took the bus to Sacred Heart.

Jacqui Childs Taliaferro

I was talking to John Spann the other day and he was telling me that he came to Sacred Heart in the 1950's. He went to some other church, one of the Polish churches and the priest told him "You don't belong here. There is a colored parish over at Sacred Heart. That's where you should go."

Judy Carty

I was coming from a place right up there by the freeway. Interstate 96 took part of that place too. I used to walk up to the streetcar stop with my son. We were right up there by a Catholic school at Woodward and Medbury. But having all white, they wouldn't take my son there so that's the reason I had to bring him down to St. Peter Claver. So the next year there was a lady that lived in the neighborhood, I've forgotten her name. She wasn't Catholic but she went up there to see if she could get her son in. And they told her that if she could find somebody that was Catholic that had a child that they would take him because there would be more than one colored. So, she came to see me and I told her, "No. They refused him before and so he will keep on going to St. Peter Claver." The young boy lived in the same building I lived in. He could go to the Catholic school off St. Antoine, but he couldn't serve on the altar. He had to come as an altar boy to Sacred Heart.

Mary Hastings

The unrelenting attacks on black people, both hidden and overt, have resulted in a fundamental worldview that interprets the behavior of others through the eyes of prejudice. What many of us do not take into consideration is that prejudice exists in virtually all of the relations between people of different cultures, ethnicities, classes, religions and any other differences that people can ascertain or imply. We are ready to believe that this worldview has had both positive and negative consequences for black people. A positive consequence for the beleaguered black people of the time was that it forced them to rely on each other, support each other and collaborate to mutual advantage. A negative outcome that became very apparent in later years was that the expectation of prejudice made many of us so suspicious of the aims of others that we became "prickly" and unable to recognize or accept well-meaning offers of support. Be that as it may, the little congregation at St. Mary's was immersed in the reality of often-violent prejudices. Their efforts are all the more notable for that reality.

Cultural and Ethnic Conflicts at Sacred Heart

In an almost eerie parallel to the situation of black people, the Italian community had begun to experience similar reactions from the Germans to their presence at Sacred Heart. In 1922, the German population in the community surrounding their beloved parish church had declined significantly. Concurrently, the Italian population had increased. The Germans were under pressure from the Diocese to relinquish the church to the Italians. In an impassioned plea to the

Diocese in the form of a lengthy letter, the Germans argued for their right to retain the Sacred Heart church for their use. The Diocese agreed and allowed the Germans to retain the structure. But, the twin pressures of German flight and Italian influx made the turnover inevitable.

To show how black people have no monopoly on presumed prejudice, we offer an excerpt from a document written to the Diocese from Mother M. Stanislas Kostka, the Mother Superior of the Sisters of Notre Dame at their convent in Milwaukee, Wisconsin. This letter was dated June 21, 1922. The letter was written to the Rt. Rev. M. J. Gallagher, D. D. at the Bishop's residence in Detroit. Bear in mind that the letter to the Diocese from the parishioners at Sacred Heart that we cited earlier was dated March 20, 1922.

> "As we are in such great need of teachers that we are obliged to withdraw from a few schools in order to meet the requirements for September, I am writing to inform you that we wish to recall the Sisters from the Sacred Heart School, Detroit. Conditions and circumstances there are so well known to Your Lordship that I need not enter into any explanation of why we think our withdrawal will cause you little or no embarrassment.
>
> The relations between the people of the parish and the Sisters during the past forty-six years have been all that we could desire and we are truly grateful for all kindnesses received."
> Sacred Heart Archives

We are fascinated by the delicate manner in which the Mother Superior addresses the turmoil at Sacred Heart. "Conditions and circumstances there are so well known to Your Lordship that I need not enter into any explanation of why we think our withdrawal will cause you little or no embarrassment." Clearly Mother Kostka is aware of the German reaction to the Italians. We can also assert with some confidence that she feels secure in her decision to withdraw. What we are left to surmise is why she felt so secure in her decision. We wish to examine our assumptions in some detail because these will inform our interpretations of what happened to the St. Peter Claver congregation during subsequent events at Sacred Heart.

We assume that the length of the relationship between the religious order and the congregation that it serves has a strong, positive effect. Mother Kostka is obviously pleased that the Sisters had served the parish for forty-six years and enjoyed the "kindnesses received."

We assume that the strong attachments that had been developed between the German parishioners and the religious order had quite a lot to do with the decision to withdraw when the Italians arrived.

We assume that the letter was a written confirmation of an understanding between Mother Kostka and Bishop Gallagher that had probably been reached in previous conversations. The brevity of the letter suggests that Mother Kostka and the Bishop agreed that the "conditions and circumstances" at the parish were such that a strategic withdrawal was prudent.

We cannot be so sure of what it means that the "withdrawal will cause you little or no embarrassment." We offer a very tentative assumption. The Bishop was apparently caught on the horns of a difficult dilemma. Does he support the Germans in their highly impassioned defense of their ownership rights? Does he support the Italians in their need for a church home in their neighborhood? Does he defy social reality and insist that the Germans and Italians share the church? We can only guess at how the conflict played itself out. What we do know is that the Germans could hold out only just so long against the inevitability of community change.

The assumptions we have offered are based on our observations of how organizations such as religious orders as well as the Catholic Church operate. Values and mission provide the energy to keep the organization going. Rules, regulations and procedures hold the faithful together and define the practices that make the religious order or the Church itself what they are. Too often, social realities force the office holders to make dreadful choices between what the organization stands for and what it must do to survive.

We offer this view of cultural and ethnic conflict in Sacred Heart to show that racism involving black and white is just a more virulent and visible form of an ongoing pattern of relations among any set of varied cultures when their members are not eternally vigilant.

The Dreadful Choices

The racism exhibited within the Church reflected the brutal reality of life for black people in America.

Catholicism in the South was a mirror reflection of the society at the time. Parishes, schools, seminaries and Catholic universities were just as segregated as the rest of America. Southern bishops did not have the fortitude to stand up to white parishioners and invite a black priest or nun to work in the region. These prelates believed that segregation could prevent turmoil. When the Vatican inquired about their stance, their response was that the Holy See would do well to understand the racial distinctions in the US. The Catholic Church did not make them and could not resolve them.

The American bishops had given up attempting to combat the vicious, ongoing racism. However, the Pope and the Holy See, to their credit, had not given up. In fact, Pope Benedict XV scolded missionaries in the US for putting national values above religious values. These national values had placed severe burdens on the teachings of the Church.

We have evidence that members of the clergy were quite comfortable exercising their prejudices. An activist, Saul Alinsky, began organizing in the late 1930's. He supported the powerless in defending themselves against the powerful. As a side note, Alinsky's work with the downtrodden made him rather cynical about ultimate outcomes. He asserted that when the powerless became powerful, they would be just as vicious as the people they replaced. That did not deter him from continuing his very valuable work. In Chicago he observed that members of the clergy had little regard for their fellow priests. A *Washington Post* reporter apparently agreed when he wrote that Lithuanians thought of Poles as enemies, the Slovaks felt the same about the Bohemians, the Germans were suspected by all of those. The Jews were out of the question and the Irish considered everyone else to be a foreigner.

The Pope and some bishops attempted to overcome this emphasis on nationality and ethnicity by establishing what were called national churches. That is, churches that were uniquely American and welcoming to all nationalities and ethnicities. These efforts were fought bitterly by other bishops, clergy and their parishioners. In fact, the attempt only strengthened the resolve of the various nationalities by giving them a sense of shared victimization.

Given the reluctance of the vast majority of bishops and clergy to confront the issue, the Church in effect, withdrew into a self-protective mode by accommodating the white Catholics. This undeniable loss for the Pope and the Holy See makes clear how the Church functions. The Bishop of Rome, the Pope, is to all intents and purposes, a bishop. He is equivalent to other bishops except when he speaks "ex cathedra," in the name of the Church and through the power of God. The Pope cannot use this power indiscriminately without severe damage to Peter's Throne. In other words, the Pope would not demand obedience from the US bishops unless he was certain that he could make the demand stick.

Given the strength of the US bishops, the Pope knew that demanding that they do something about the treatment of black people would be a losing battle. He had no credible threat to hold them in line. Then, as now, the US bishops hold great sway over the Church. The power of any bishop is directly proportional to the wealth of the diocese for which the bishop is responsible. In this way, the Church operates just as any other large, multinational organization. US bishops wield disproportionate influence relative to European and Third World bishops precisely because of the vast wealth at their disposal in US dioceses.

The US bishops were clearly responding to their constituencies, the parishes that made up the dioceses. Only when Dr. Martin Luther King, Jr. and the civil rights movement began to turn the tide of public opinion did the US bishops find their consciences.

We thank Leslie Tentler[4] for much of the following information that we gleaned about the choices facing the religious at this tumultuous time in Detroit's history.

45

Bishop Michael Gallagher was among those who made a serious effort to help before it became somewhat acceptable to do so. St. Peter Claver Parish had been in operation since 1911. In 1927, Bishop Gallagher gave permission to establish a second parish for black Catholics. There were those at the time who believed that the growing number of black Catholics was the reason for the additional parish. However, the number of black Catholics was still quite small. The reason for the second parish had more to do with the appointment by Bishop Gallagher of Father Norman Dukette to the Diocese. As the first black priest to serve in the Diocese, Father Dukette had the responsibility to serve as missionary to Detroit's increasing population of southern black migrants. Bishop Gallagher did not want to send Father Dukette to St. Peter Claver. That would have been unfair to the Holy Ghost Fathers who had cared for St. Peter Claver from its inception. To assign Father Dukette to one of the white parishes would have inflamed the parishioners. By default, St. Benedict the Moor parish was chosen as the start for Father Dukette's career.

We are impressed with the fact that Bishop Gallagher had to take great pains to circumvent the influence of his white parishioners in his efforts to support both the black Catholic population and his own black priest. Bishop Gallagher also had to be politically conscious of his relationship with the Holy Ghost Fathers. Again we are made aware of how much the Church functions like a large corporation or any other political body when it must balance the demands of its several constituencies.

Leslie Tentler[14] informs us that in 1917, black Catholics in Washington, D.C formed a "Committee Against the Extension of Race Prejudice in the Church." They objected to discriminatory practices in some congregations, the lack of schools for black Catholics and the lack of black priests. The fact that the committee made these charges indicated that there was, even at that time, a racial awareness and a latent militancy among black people. By the 1940's this militancy was a good deal more evident than before. That reality posed special

---

[14] Op. Cit., p. 500

problems for black Catholics. Since parish priests were subject either to an order or to a Bishop, loyalty to black people often meant disloyalty to the Church. Even a moderate group, the Federated Colored Catholics at St. Benedict the Moor which sought to bring a black priest to the parish was rebuffed by the Chancery. The Chancellor, Edward Hickey, told one petitioner, "Loyal parishioners should be willing to support their church financially and to endeavor to give enthusiastic backing to the plans which the Pastor adopts for its welfare." He was not moved by the complaint that the Holy Ghost Fathers were not progressive.[15]

This account contains a wealth of information important to us. We understand that the Church body was, in many places and circumstances, discriminatory. Even moderate attempts at change were discouraged. Attempts to bring a black priest to the parish had been rebuffed by the Chancery. Even at that, we were quite unprepared for the bombshell statement that "the Holy Ghost Fathers were not progressive." Our persistent and effective congregation had to overcome some barriers that we would not have predicted.

The parishioners at St. Peter Claver knew that Bishop Gallagher was entertaining the thought of installing Father Dukette at St. Peter Claver. The situation had to have been difficult for Bishop Gallagher as well as Father Charles Kapp, pastor since 1924. Father Kapp was held in high regard by the parishioners and had been very effective in increasing the number of baptisms. But, clearly, there were quite a few parishioners who hoped that Father Dukette would become pastor. We have not been able to find the reason why the Holy Ghost Fathers were believed to be unprogressive.

Father Dukette spent a year after his ordination traveling, with the ostensible purpose of surveying the progress of Catholicism among black people. There is some indication that this travel had an alternative purpose, that is, to give Bishop Gallagher time to find a place for him. The effort paid off when Father Dukette was given the new parish of St. Benedict the Moor. In response to the demands of the time, the new church had been designated as a racial parish,

---

[15]   Sacred Heart Archives

its members to be drawn from the black population on the west side of Detroit. The numbers of black Catholics were smaller than on the east side, but wealthier. Typically, the parish remained biracial for a time.

But, even under these rather fortuitous circumstances, the pressures on the Church hierarchy had to have been intense. The white families that attended St. Benedict were typical in that they lived in the neighborhood and went there because of its convenience. The relatively wealthy black people were little threat to them. The priest, Father Dukette, was probably polished and welcoming. Leslie Tentler[16] tells us that a typical Sunday Mass was evenly divided with about 60 blacks and a similar number of whites. The problem is why the count was taken at the time. It seems that there was a white committee formed to persuade the Chancery of the need for an English speaking church in the neighborhood. "English speaking" was code for white. They did not want to share the church with black people, even comparatively wealthy ones. Under pressure, the Chancery was forced to respond. It did so with a ruling reiterating that St. Benedict was a racial parish and that whites were not parishioners in the usual sense of the term. That was the beginning of the exodus of the remaining whites from St. Benedict.

What the white people failed to realize then as well as now, is that black people do not depend on the participation of whites to be successful. In spite of its lack of resources and the dwindling number of whites, St. Benedict grew rapidly. In just over a year, Father Dukette enjoyed 103 conversions. Most of these were black children. Father Dukette hoped to reach adults, parents and other family members, through the children. The pattern was that black parishes generally grew rapidly once the parish established a school.

Unfortunately, Father Dukette did not remain at St. Benedict the Moor. He was removed from the parish and assigned, in October of 1929, to found a "colored mission" in Flint, Michigan. The city had only a small black population and a history of anti-Catholicism. This clearly punitive move apparently resulted from some serious offense

---

[16] Op. Cit., p. 503

for which Bishop Gallagher had found Father Dukette guilty. The Chancery archives do not provide information on the nature of the offense. However, Father Dukette remained effective even under the trying circumstances he found in Flint. We understand that many black Catholics who had him as pastor have been making a serious effort to begin the beatification process for him.

We want to emphasize a serious point raised in this account which could cause some confusion. The numbers of black Catholics in the city at that time did not warrant a second parish. St. Benedict the Moor was established to accommodate a black priest who could not be assigned elsewhere. That priest, Father Norman Dukette, was to be a missionary to the black population of Detroit. This second parish then, was opened to spearhead the increase in the number of black Catholics rather than to support growing numbers. This theme was to be repeated in the opening of Sacred Heart to black Catholics. Even though the St. Peter Claver congregation outgrew its quarters and there was a need for more space, there was another reason for the choice of Sacred Heart as the next parish home. Father Thiefels and Mother De Sales were both confident that opening Sacred Heart to their black parishioners, students and parents would attract the "better class of colored people" to the parish and school from the nearby projects. This would, in turn, increase the likelihood of success in increasing the number of black Catholics for the Church. If we are correct in our assessment of Church motivations at this time, we feel confident in our later assessment. When it closes predominantly black parishes in the present day, the Church, in effect, abandons its efforts to minister to black Catholics.

Prejudice Within the Black Community

We have observed that the Catholic Church was a beacon of light to the black community at this time in US history. There was another factor that made the Church attractive to some of us. That factor was a form of prejudice involving both class and color within the black community. We are alerted to the impact of this phenomenon by the comments from Father Thiefels and Mother De Sales that Sacred Heart would attract, "the better class of colored people."

We are pained to acknowledge the reality of black-on-black prejudice, but it has had such a profound effect on our relations with each other as well as with the larger world that we must confront its consequences forthrightly. The origins of this prejudice appear to be embedded in the fearsome brutality of white people against black people. There are always members of the victimized who will rage and fight against the oppressor. There are others who will hunker down and avoid contact with the oppressor. There are still others who will identify with the oppressor and attempt to ingratiate themselves so as to gain some distance from those who bear the brunt of the violence. This last type need not be a craven response. The very fact that one people oppresses another signifies that the oppressor has more power. There are very practical reasons for understanding the source of this oppressive power and adopting those practices that will help the individual to attain it. Those people who identify with the oppressor in many cases prefer to acquire power rather than fight those who have it.

The visible distinctions of color and class trigger the prejudices within the black community just as it does between the white and black communities. The visible distinctions include the following:

The degree to which the hair is kinky or straight.
The degree to which skin color approaches black or white.
The degree to which the person speaks using the black dialect or classical English.
The degree to which a person manifests enjoyment of cultural forms normally associated with black people or with those normally associated with white people.
The degree to which a person exhibits habits of study and learning.

While all of these distinctions can trigger some form of prejudice, skin color and hair are usually the source of the most intense and violent reactions among black people. In practice, those who most closely resemble white people generate the most immediate and intense attack.

We are from Mobile.
We come from a mixed family of light and dark skinned

> people.
> The light skinned people are Catholic.
> The children who went to Heart of Mary looked white.
> The brown children went to my grandfather's AME church.
> We were offered the opportunity to go to a Catholic school because we were going to public school and we were not reading in the fifth grade, also because we were fighting. The kids would yank our hair out.
>
> Gale Northcross

Black Prejudices and the Church

Their darker brothers and sisters often single out black people with fair skin and straight hair for attack. This happened so often in public schools that their parents were forced to find non-public schools to protect them. Catholic schools, noted for their discipline, order and focus on education fit the need nicely.

> At my school, the older boys would hold the door open for the students to enter school. One time a strange thing happened. As I was walking into school, one of the boys holding the door cut off my braid! When I got home I remember crying for a long time as my mother had to cut off the other braid to even out my hair. Needless to say, my mother took me out of that school and took me to Sacred Heart.
>
> Gloria Wright

However, there was another outcome of black-on-black prejudice that was not so obvious. Black people of all shades often heard from their parents to, "better your race." This was not-so-subtle code for marrying a person of a lighter shade than oneself and, preferably, with straighter hair. Black people who looked more like white people were known to have better opportunities and greater acceptance in the world than their darker siblings. The result was that fair skinned black people often attempted to distance themselves from dark people. The Church, again, provided a haven for them.

The Church became a haven precisely because of its perception as a religion for white people. With its solemn rituals, quiet, contemplative services, Latin language and Gregorian chanting the Church was far removed from the earthy, emotional and soul-searing services in the black churches. Black people who wanted to show that they were "not like the others," often chose Catholicism as a way to emphasize the difference.

> Black Catholics saw themselves as different from ordinary black people.
> I remember hearing a minister from Chicago who actually said, "We are better. We are CATHOLIC."
> We sounded so high and mighty when we said that.
> A few of us lived in the projects. When we walked around, here is the way we looked (she demonstrates nose-in-the-air).
> Then, when I would visit family they would say, "She goes to a CATHOLIC school. They speak Latin. Say something in Latin for us."
> When the church said, "no more Latin," they were taking one of our precious privileges.
>
> Pat Abner

A Persistent and Effective Congregation

Clearly, there were complex forces operating on the still fledgling congregation that began at St. Mary's. Beset from within and without, the members had to navigate through treacherous waters to have any chance for survival. But the opportunity to participate in a unique community drew black people to the new parish. Those who remember, describe St. Peter Claver this way:

> Our church was a place of worship, along with the school activities. Here we came together to praise God and leave with the spirit to serve one another in our community. Our dances, picnics, club meetings, choir practices and many social involvements not only made us personally concerned for each other, but they gave expression to our concerns for social improvement, political participation and spiritual depth.
>
> Church Bulletin

Significantly, the church activities "made us personally concerned for each other (and) gave expression to our concerns for social improvement, political participation and spiritual depth." We are impressed with the fact that church participation resulted in the congregation becoming active Christians. Their participation had the effect of having them to demonstrate their Christianity in every aspect of their lives. They nurtured and supported each other. They took actions to improve social conditions. They involved themselves in the political process. They were, indeed, a vibrant and effective community.

The parish, as is typical of black people who survived the assaults, had to call upon bottomless wells of patience and certainty of self-worth to sustain itself. There was precious little help from even the Church religious.

My first understanding of Catholics and the race issue was in the fourth grade. We were rooming on the west side. The only black Catholic church in the area was St. Benedict the Moor that had no school. The next closest church was St. Dominic's on Trumbull and Warren. The priest there referred my mother to Sacred Heart as he asked her, "Wouldn't you be happier with your own kind?" The next closest school was St. Leo. They took me. I didn't discover until I read some research material in 2003 that St. Leo had a quota of seven for blacks. Early Affirmative Action? I was part of their 1944 quota.

Almeta White

The priest at St. Dominic's had clearly made an assumption about the preference of black people to associate with each other. The unstated preference was just as clear that the priest did not want his parish or his school children to associate with black people. This attitude was and, perhaps, remains dominant in white parishes and schools. The St. Peter Claver congregation had to endure the consequences of such attitudes if they were to survive and prosper even with the aid of those in the Church who would minister to them.

The Impact of Church Bureaucracy

We will examine more closely what it is about the way the Church functions that produces barriers when Catholics are faced with matters of conscience. We look for an explanation for the hidden barriers by beginning with the quote from the Chancellor, Edward Hickey. "Loyal parishioners should be willing to support their

53

church financially and to endeavor to give enthusiastic backing to the plans which the Pastor adopts for its welfare." These words make excruciatingly clear the terms of the contract between the Church and the parishioners. The congregation is expected to pay up and obey. The "obedience" is owed to the Pastor who alone decides on what is best for the welfare of the congregation. Paternalism is a modern term for such an arrangement.

The Church was a good deal more powerful in the US and elsewhere in the early to mid-20th century than it was in the latter part of the century. This power was owed to the fierce loyalty of those, especially European immigrants in the US, who built their lives around the parish and its pastor. Bishops and priests ruled by fiat. Parishioners took quite seriously threats of hell, mortal sin, heresy and excommunication from the body of Christ. This gave the clergy remarkable control over their parishes.

The control over the clergy by the Church hierarchy was even more remarkable. Religious who took seriously their vows of poverty and obedience supported the spiritual mission of the Church. Bishops were able to send their religious into what amounted to battle with utmost assurance that their soldiers would perform under sometimes-intense fire.

The spiritual mission of the Church was, and is, at times undermined by the temporal mission. The temporal mission is to survive as a functioning and effective organization. To survive requires that the Church be able to sustain its troops as well as its material holdings. This requirement to sustain itself requires the acquisition and expenditure of tremendous sums of money. Difficulties arise when the two missions become incompatible. The need to serve the needs of those who will pay can, and does, subvert the spiritual mission to serve those who cannot pay. We have already seen how the need to satisfy various racial and ethnic groups often ran counter to the demands of Christ-like behavior. We will investigate, in due course, how this conflict affected, and still affects, the question of closing churches and redistributing their parishioners.

We will focus first on the soldiers, the priests and nuns who interact daily with the faithful as the visible face of the Church. We put ourselves, as much as we can, in their shoes as the bishop asks them to be missionaries to the black community.

Information from the archives does not spell out the attitudes, but we can get a sense of the likelihood from what the archives do say. St. Mary's black congregation was designated as a "mission." This designation remained through St. Peter Claver and Sacred Heart. This congregation and subsequently, that of St. Benedict the Moor, was to spearhead the mission to the black community.

There are at least two connotations of the word "mission." The first is rather benign. One or more religious will be sent out from the order to engage in a set of tasks to achieve a purpose. This connotation is similar to a military campaign in which soldiers are ordered to accomplish the mission. The second connotation is loaded with negative baggage. From it we get a picture of noble and enlightened religious who sacrifice themselves to work among those who are not capable of taking care of themselves. Their task is to uplift the ignorant and, somehow, make them presentable, that is, more like their superiors, more like white people.

We have some indication that, among the religious who worked in the black community, both connotations were present. There were those who respected black people and sought to help relieve the intolerable pressures put upon them. There were also those who harbored beliefs about black inferiority and sought to ennoble themselves by providing aid and comfort to the helpless creatures.

Black people were often very much aware of the distinctions among the religious. Black people would love the one and tolerate the other.

In the following chapter, we will take a close look at the religious who worked with the fledgling congregation, the students and the parents.

CHAPTER FOUR
The Missionaries

The work of Dr. Martin Luther King, Jr. inspired the song, *We Shall Overcome.* We believe that black people have been overcoming ever since the Middle Passage. The congregation that began at St. Mary's demonstrated for us the day-to-day struggles that allowed our people to survive and even prosper. But, the struggle would undoubtedly have been a lot more difficult, if not impossible, without appropriate help at crucial points. We found in Sacred Heart's archives a chronicle that offers a brief timeline of the important points in the congregation's history.

Recall that Old St. Mary's offered the first refuge for the congregation in 1911. Father Joseph Wuest, C. S. Sp., formed the St. Peter Claver Aid Society from members of St. Mary's parish. Bear in mind that those contributing members were white people. The Aid Society raised sufficient funds to purchase an Episcopal Church in 1914. That church became St. Peter Claver.

In 1914, Father Francis Wermers, C. S. Sp., left $1000 to the "St. Peter Claver Colored Mission" in his will. That money was used by Father Kreutzkamph, pastor, to purchase an apartment building in 1917. That apartment building became the St. Peter Claver School and rectory. "Through Father Kreutzkamph's truly heroic efforts, the parish was brought to good financial standing. In 1924, he paid off many debts and with the cooperation of his parishioners, managed to leave a neat sum of money." This statement from the archives leaves no doubt that the parishioners were not standing by idly while the priests did all of the work. However, that does not detract from the reality that dedicated, self-sacrificing priests led the way for a congregation that desperately needed hard working leadership.

The parish certainly had to be grateful for the dedication of the Holy Ghost priests. The next pastor, Father Kapp was appointed in 1924. The archives inform us that Father Kapp burned the mortgage on the rectory in 1926 and in 1927 started a building fund for the school. The parish can reasonably trace its growth to the advent of the school building effort. We are aware that the number of converts to the Church rises rapidly once a parish establishes a school.

The skillful and self-sacrificing work of the Holy Ghost fathers was continued with the remarkable success of Father Henry Thiefels who was appointed pastor in 1932. God's providence was evident in the fortuitous combination of Bishop Gallagher and Father Thiefels. Bishop Gallagher had been appointed to the Detroit Diocese in 1918. Having built a number of churches and schools, he had long wanted a school for the beleaguered black children.

We know that Bishop Gallagher sought the services of an order of nuns to teach in such a school, but without success for some time. The depression beginning with the stock market crash of 1929 clearly had a lot to do with the fact that the nuns he asked were reluctant to supply the needed service without remuneration. What other factors might have been involved in their refusal would be the subject of mere speculation. What has been reported is the acceptance of the opportunity by the Felician nuns. One report has it that in the spring of 1936, Mother de Sales of the Felician order had been wishing to do real missionary work and saw an opportunity right on her doorstep, so to speak. She saw the little colored children playing on the street outside of the convent on St. Aubin and Canfield streets. She called on the Bishop and offered her sisters for a school at St. Peter Claver's church.

This rather frank admission that work among black people in the US amounted to domestic missionary work would shape the efforts in ways that were both helpful and harmful to the nuns' black charges. Again we point out that both of the religious orders that offered their support, the Holy Ghost fathers and the Felician nuns were devoted to missionary work. Both would have their values and ideals severely tested in the ostensibly civilized society of the US.

Felician Sisters Of St. Peter Claver

The archives of the Felician Sisters at their motherhouse in Livonia, Michigan produced a colorful portrait of what it was like for them to serve the parish. Their participation began quietly enough.

Rt. Rev. Bishop Michael Gallagher, Ordinary of the Detroit Archdiocese, had long planned to open a school for the Catholic Negro children. However, the financial lack made the realization of this project very difficult. Several attempts to solicit help from various Religious Communities in procuring at least two teaching sisters to take over the school were without result.

One Sunday, Monsignor S. Woznicki confided this concern to Mother M. De Sales, Provincial Superior of the Felician Sisters. She was touched with pity. Mother De Sales presented the issue to her Provincial Councilors. They wholeheartedly supported Mother De Sales' plan to send sisters to staff the school.

The General Superior, Mother Mary Pia, gladly approved the plan. The Felician Sisters sent two sisters to work with the Negro children of St. Peter Claver without remuneration. The sisters would commute daily from the Motherhouse on Canfield and St. Aubin in Detroit.

Felician Archives[17]

We know that at least part of Mother de Sales motivation was her first-hand picture of the plight of the black children in her neighborhood. We can imagine that another part of her motivation was to provide her sisters with an opportunity to do "real missionary work" without having to send them around the globe. We have no explicit knowledge of what the nuns thought about being missionaries in terms of their attitudes toward the children and their parents. We can deduce from the prevailing attitudes what is likely to have been in their minds. The fact that they were highly trained and sincerely motivated to do the work that God had called them to do could not insulate them entirely from the corrosive atmosphere of the time.

Father Henry Thiefels played an important role in helping Bishop Gallagher to meet his objective. We have reproduced a letter from Father Thiefels to the bishop that requests the school.

---

[17] We are grateful to Sister Elaine, current archivist at the Felician Motherhouse in Livonia, Michigan for supplying us with the documents that we have used for this and subsequent descriptions from the Felician archives.

June 2, 1936

Most Rev. Michael J. Gallagher, D. D.
Bishop of Detroit Diocese

Detroit, Mich.

Most Rev. and Dear Bishop:

I am sending to your Excellency some observations I have made in the past few years for your consideration. They pertain to the establishment of a school for St. Peter Claver (colored) Parish. I sincerely believe them to be correct and I have no biased view in the matter, leaving everything to your final judgment.

I have observed that (on enclosed map) the section bounded in red is 85% to 90% colored population. 90% of the children in public school are colored. A large portion of white children in Sacred Heart School are Italian. There is a white Italian school nearby. 85% of children in St. Wenceslaus School are colored. There is a question whether St. Wenceslaus School will open in September because of a preponderance of colored children. This would put these children back in public schools, many of which have gone to the Catholic school from the first grade. Also, many of them are converts. Forty of them have made their First Communion in my Parish in the last two years with express written permission of parents and a written promise that they will raise them Catholics. The trustees tried to close St. Wenceslaus School last year. This knowledge is based on a conversation with the Sisters.

The Government is going ahead with the new housing project for the colored and will be completed within the year. Sacred Heart Church and School is located in the best possible position to draw from all sides the people who are interested in the Catholic Faith. There are many who are interested, but are shy to come here because the present St. Peter Claver is so small and they would be noticed.

I have had many inquiries about a Catholic school for the children of colored parents. The better class of colored do not want to send their children to the public schools which at present have anything but a moral background. From these facts it would seem that a school for St. Peter Claver would be a grave necessity. Divine Providence coming to your Excellencies rescue has given us the Sisters needed, etc.

I, therefore humbly ask your Excellency permission to open a school for St. Peter Claver Parish in the coming Fall. This school could be located temporarily in the apartment house, now known as the Rectory and property of the Diocese. If it is not possible to obtain Sacred Heart Church and School for the present, at least we can carry on until sentiment can be aroused to make the people who are holding out in Sacred Heart to realize that they are retarding the spread of the Catholic Faith.

Ever your humble servant
In Spiritu Sancto
Henry P. Thiefels, C. S. Sp.
Pastor

Sacred Heart Archives

This letter gives us important information about the situation that Bishop Gallagher and Father Thiefels faced. St. Wenceslaus had too many black children and was threatening to close. Sacred Heart was not yet open to black children even though the neighborhood was up to 90% black. St. Peter Claver School was a stopgap measure to protect the children until Sacred Heart would be available.

We consider ourselves fortunate to have available in the archives a description provided by the first nuns who were assigned to the "new mission school of St. Peter Claver." They were Sister Mary Angelica and Sister Mary Pulcheria. The school year was 1936 – 1937.

In order to become acquainted with the locality and to present ourselves to the Pastor as the teachers in the newly planned school, we set out on the 22nd of August for the Parish of St. Peter Claver. We heard of the locality from others. Upon reaching the area, we looked around for a building resembling a school. Finally, we spotted a large apartment house directly across from a neatly kept church. There was only one entrance to the building. Hesitating, we climbed up a littered stairway, but met no one. We stood a moment perplexed. Could this cluttered building be the living quarters of the Pastor? A moment later, the riddle was solved. These were the rooms the workers were remodeling into the classrooms, while on the other side we spotted a door marked "Office."

Father Thiefels returned soon and made us welcome. He was delighted to see us. He gave us his blessing and pleaded with us not to change our minds concerning our dedication to teach the children at his Parish school. We agreed to join the celebration of the Sunday Mass.

Entering the church, we were impressed by the piety of the people. Most of them, upon entering, both young and old, lingered at the large crucifix, touching the feet of Jesus and with bowed heads gave reverence to the Savior. Others were praying the Stations of the Cross. Among them we spotted a little girl, no more than 7, who gazed upon the Stations as if in a trance. Even when we passed her, she was not distracted, but continued praying.

The church was clean and orderly. Boys followed by men occupied the right side of the aisle. The left side, girls, followed by women. The sparkling, inquisitive eyes of the children followed our every move. The Pastor asked the parishioners to show their kindness to the Sisters in all ways. He urged them to appreciate the work of the Sisters and to remember them in their prayers. He then turned to the Children of Mary and encouraged them to offer their Holy Communion for the Felician Sisters and the entire congregation. Many of the worshippers approached the Lord's Table and received Holy Communion with great reverence.

We left with mixed feelings of sympathy and admiration for these poor and discriminated, unfairly treated people. Our first visit in the Church left us with an overpowering gratitude to God that He chose us to be the first missionaries to these, the least of the little ones. Initially we felt an apprehension and fear, but after several days we felt in this new apostolate a strong bond of attachment and love for these dark skinned among whom we wished to work and to whom we intended to bring the Word of God. They, like we, belong to God's fold and differ from us only in outer color.

Felician Archives

From this heartfelt description we learn a great deal about the two courageous women who accepted, with honor and dignity, an assignment that would be extremely difficult at best. Their character and devotion is obvious in their expression of "overpowering gratitude to God that He chose us to be the first missionaries to these, the least of the little ones." The conditions that they faced had to have been clearly obvious given their initial feelings of "apprehension and fear."

We get a clear indication of the part that the congregation played when we understand that it took just "several days" for them to feel a "strong bond of attachment." Father Thiefels must have done a good job of making the congregation aware of the sacrifice that the nuns were making to teach in the school. He was also well aware of the nature of the task he was asking the nuns to take on. He "pleaded with us not to change our minds." He was obviously afraid that having seen the conditions, the nuns might not be willing to follow through with the mission. However, just like true soldiers, the nuns' commitment was secure. Their description of the piety expressed by the people must have been extended to the personal relations between the nuns and the people. The people were indeed grateful for the help and probably did all that they could reasonably do to make the nuns feel welcome and safe.

We will emphasize, once again, how the intense faith and piety of the black parishioners contributed to their survival and to their ultimate success. Here we have evidence from the missionaries themselves that the people were not just passive recipients of aid, but active in sharing with the nuns in a collaborative effort. This notion of collaboration will be repeated often in this story. It is one of the principle values that continue to support the Sacred Heart family.

The narrative that Sisters Angelica and Pulcheria provided continues:

> School registration for the 1936-1937 school year took place on September 8th. For the first time, delighted mothers hurried to enroll their children not only in a Catholic school, but also in their own Catholic school. What a joyful experience it was when 64 children gathered within the school walls the following day. They filled two classrooms, most coming from Catholic families. Each day the number of children increased because even non-Catholics pleaded to accept their children in order to secure them a good education and sound moral upbringing. They requested that their children be allowed to

participate in Religion classes along with the others, and that they may accept the Catholic faith if their conscience would so guide them.

The first day was spent in the parish hall in the church basement since the classrooms had not yet been completed. The hall was not well ventilated and not equipped to serve as a classroom. Therefore, trying to teach a disorganized group of 64 new students was extremely difficult. This situation lasted three weeks and was both very taxing and demanding much ingenuity on the part of the teaching sisters.

Finally, the sisters decided to join the 2 separate grade levels into one group and start with teaching the basics of good conduct. They began with drilling the children to walk in lines, to stand, kneel, sit and respond politely. As time went on, this restless, unruly group began to adjust to the demands of proper conduct. A few adjustments were made and then teaching began to advance more smoothly and the children worked diligently.

Felician Archives

First Class, 1936

The nuns' report indicates the absolute necessity of good order before learning takes place. This emphasis on order, polite response and proper conduct is what distinguished a Catholic education under the nuns from public education. The parents played a strong part in the imposition of these values. A call to a parent about an uncooperative child would be followed with stern discipline for the child. The word of the nun was golden and not to be countered with excuses. Only obedience was acceptable. The degree of success was made apparent to Father Thiefels at Mass.

> A month after the opening of the school, Father Thiefels left for a two-week rest at the Community Motherhouse in Pittsburgh. Upon his return, we noticed that Father turned around and surveyed the church several times during the Mass. We wondered what was wrong. Before beginning the homily, Father said, "From the time school opened until my departure, it seemed to me that I was offering Mass in a circus, but now, to my great surprise, it's so quiet and peaceful in the church. I was afraid that all of our little ones must have slipped away from church and gone home. I kept turning around just to be sure I'm not the only one left. However, I noticed that they were all there, praying devoutly. Now you can see what a good Catholic upbringing can accomplish."

Felician Archives

We thrill at the words, "A good Catholic education." In the short space of two weeks, a collaborative effort between parents and nuns had produced the essential conditions for learning. The result was a set of values, based upon discipline, which led not only to learning, but also to devout prayer.

The situation that the nuns faced was appalling. Their report reveals both the conditions that they had to overcome and the stoicism and determination that made them successful.

> All beginnings are difficult; ours was no exception. The classrooms were ready, but totally lacking in everything; books, maps, charts, chalk, erasures, pencils, paper, and all other equipment. Additional children were requesting admission continually. How could we refuse? Every soul is a valuable

gem, purchased by Christ with His own blood, waiting to be carved, shaped and treasured.

We finally came up with a solution to the problem. Perhaps we could solicit help from the many schools that our Sisters staffed. Mother Mary DeSales approved our plan and we set out to beg for assistance. To our delight, all Principals and Convent Superiors responded generously. We were received kindly wherever we went and were swamped with various school supplies. Even the girls at the Felician Academy and Home for Children shared with us whatever they had on hand. May the good Lord reward all our benefactors most generously.

The news that the Felician Sisters opened a Mission School for black children at St. Peter Claver spread with the speed of lightning and caused a flurry of interest. Even the newspapers carried commentaries on this new venture. Consequently, other schools and churches began sending something for the children, especially around the holidays.

Felician Archives

This rather matter of fact recitation is both heartwarming and heartbreaking. The sisters had to beg and they did. Their sisters responded generously. Their noble work was even newsworthy. Who can now imagine what it must have been like for the first black Catholic congregation in the state of Michigan to become newsworthy because nuns decided to help? The neglect from all other sources other than Felician nuns and Holy Ghost priests had to have been deeply ingrained in society.

The story that the nuns told offers another look at how the congregation took advantage of a clear opportunity. Black people who were there can attest to the importance that was placed on education by the black community. The often-spoken words were, "They can't take your education from you." White people might take everything else, but not your education. The nuns did a remarkable job. Black parents also did a remarkable job. Even non-Catholics "pleaded for admission."

The German Farewell

Under the most trying circumstances, the religious and parents had accomplished the near impossible. They had protected the children while imparting valuable skills and knowledge. Their perseverance was about to pay off. In August of 1938, the Pastor and German parishioners at Sacred Heart finally gave in. We will reproduce a portion of the Farewell Address from the Pastor, Father Hubert Frank Klenner, to the parishioners to show the remarkable state of mind governing the time.

FAREWELL ADDRESS
To the
Parishioners of Sacred Heart Church
August 2, 1938

In the Providence of God the day which is to terminate our happy relation as pastor and flock has come. It was, I assure you, a genuine pleasure for me to be engaged in this work for the past 16 years among you. The change in administration is due solely and simply to the inability of the parish as at present constituted to maintain it financially. For the past 8 years the school was kept in operation by the generosity of the St. Vincent de Paul Society. Your candle bill for the last six years was paid by private charity. Even in the convent large requirements were provided by outside friends and relatives of the Sisters. I kept matters going in the hope that the slum-clearance project would bring into the parish new members in sufficient numbers to revive it. However, the civil authorities have definitely decided that no whites would be accepted. On the contrary, this entire section of the town will be reserved for the colored population. I am told that the second part of this project will take in the territory east of Hastings to the railroad – from Brewster to Mack, while the third part will go north of Mack to Canfield, so that in ten years there will be no white people in this locality.

In the meantime and for the present, this church will remain your church as it was in the past. St. Peter Claver will continue as the colored mission and Mass will be said there as ever before. There will be several missionaries attached to this post and only the overflow of colored Catholics will be accommodated as guests in this church in such a way that they will neither interfere with nor inconvenience you in the least.

You will keep on attending Sacred Heart Church as long as you live in the vicinity and will be properly cared for.

In the school, the change is only in the personnel of the teachers. The white children will be accommodated first and as has been our policy in the past. If place was available, we took the colored applicants. This policy is to continue until you of your own accord leave this neighborhood. As to the societies and the use of German for those who still require it, please note that most members of the Holy Ghost Order are your own flesh and blood and it is preposterous to think that these devoted men would for one instant neglect their own kind.

Sacred Heart Archives

We leave to you the task of explaining how a priest of the Catholic Church could have such deep and passionate concern for his white parishioners and so little regard, perhaps even disdain and contempt, for their darker brothers and sisters. The implications are so terrifying that again we are forced to delve into our nightmares to imagine what life must have been like for black people.

Sacred Heart

The move from St. Peter Claver to Sacred Heart was done in procession. Times had changed, so there was no fanfare, no fife and bugle corps, no divisions of marchers. However, we can relish the joy the congregation must have felt to have gained access to a beautiful church complete with rectory, convent and school. The congregation had found a home. The Archdiocese of Detroit also had a new Archbishop, Edward Mooney. We wonder how much the congregation and the Archbishop knew about what the Felician sisters had in store for them.

Original Sacred Heart frame school between church and rectory, 1875

Rectory and Convent

There were eight nuns who staffed the school. Sister Mary Pulcheria was Superior. The others were Sisters Angelica, Casimir, DePorres, Elmira, Severine, Gregory and Gilbert. They reported on their experience.

> We arrived here on the 29th of August, each one with a strong determination to be of service to the children and in any capacity to the parish. The condition of the convent upset us greatly, however. It was dirty and filled with cockroaches, bedbugs, and all kinds of other insects. The kitchen was

69

especially dirty. The sisters began cleaning energetically until late that night.

> The needs were great, as there was no food and no money. No one complained however, thanking God that He allowed us to be initiated into Mission Life right at the start. We trusted in the Divine Providence and knew He would help us. Indeed, help came sooner than we expected. Several good souls appeared as Samaritans, bringing some food. Help began to arrive from the parents of the sisters, some Superiors of other Felician convents and our sisters who began to visit us two or three times a week sharing donated food.
>
> Felician Archives

This sad recitation goes on to explain how Mother DeSales arranged to send beds and mattresses so the nuns could sleep at night. An unnamed visitor, apparently from the parish, suggested that they have the house fumigated. Having no money, they had to rely on Father Thiefels to pay the cost. The report continues with a description of registration day at the school.

> A large group of mothers already waited at the school doors. There was some confusion at the registration because the mothers of white children demanded that their children be separated from the blacks. An argument began between the two groups and a Negro woman shouted, "We, too, are God's children!" We prayed that this segregation issue would die down. It did. At registration there were 30 Black students enrolled and 90 white. Not all are Catholics.
>
> The 1938-1939 School Year opened on September 12th. We were very apprehensive, expecting some negative demonstration from the white women. Thank God, there was none. However, the children's conduct was very disturbing, both in school and in the church. There was talking, laughing, pushing and other negative antics in church. We drilled and practiced day after day. Eventually, a few of the children were dismissed from school due to incorrigibility, with approval from the Pastor.
>
> Felician Archives

The discipline, hard work and charming innocence of these pioneering women give great insight into how they were able to accomplish their mission. Their faith was their source of strength and, according to the next part of their report, they were amply rewarded for their patience and perseverance. From our point of view, their rewards were the bare minimum to sustain health, but the nuns were delighted and grateful. We offer the following paragraph from their report to illustrate.

> It is a known fact that we live from donations of kind people since we receive no remuneration for our work. It is not easy to live without some cash on hand, but God's loving Providence surrounds us. God inspires someone to share with us. Even sisters from other communities come to our aid now and then. On the Feast of St. Nicholas, for instance, the Immaculate Heart of Mary Sisters encouraged their students to bring canned food to share with us. Consequently, they presented us with 150 cans of vegetables and fruit. Several Women's Organizations have rendered help in either purchasing some household item or sending food. We never needed to stretch our hand to beg for food or money, but in some miraculous way both are provided to care for our needs. Deo gratias!

Felician Archives

It is that last "Deo gratias" that brings a lump to the throat and mist to the eyes. These women of God took their mission as seriously as soldiers on a battlefield. They were, and remain, truly inspiring.

Their report concludes with descriptions of several events that drew large crowds of both black people and white people. The events were successful due to the energy that the nuns put into "drill and practice" to prepare the children. They continued to describe the generosity of even total strangers to both themselves and to the children. The report concludes with these lines, "Our Christmas holidays passed swiftly amid joy and a bit of relaxation. The only thing we missed were the familiar, beautiful Polish Christmas Carols." This last line reminds us quite forcefully that here were women far removed from their comfort zone. Instead of their beloved Poland, they found themselves among Italians, Germans and African-Americans, housed in brutally unkind living quarters and dependent on the generosity of others to eat. For these women we, too, say with great humility and awe, "Deo gratias!"

Memories of the Missionaries

We were delighted to be granted the opportunity to interview several of the Felician Sisters who taught at Sacred Heart at one time or another. They recalled for us their time at the school and parish. We offer some of their comments here and the remainder in the Addendum.

> We had 100% cooperation from the parents.
> All we had to do was call and the mother would say, "I will be there in 20 minutes."
>
> Sister Arthur
>
> The children were polite, attentive and intelligent, obedient and happy. (There was general laughter at "obedient.") At that time it was easy.
> I enjoyed the singing of Clarence Hightower.
> It was my first experience. It was wonderful.
>
> Sister Leonette
>
> Sister Lucille always had the front door locked because of the area that we were in.
> Whenever the ladies would have something going on in the church, they made sure that we got some of that real good food.
>
> Sister Eleanor Marie

These brief comments emphasize the points we make. The parents were cooperative. The children responded to the care. The conditions the nuns faced were difficult at best.

The recollections offered by the nuns who taught at Sacred Heart give us exceedingly valuable insight into the thinking and perceptions of those who were sent, as missionaries, to help the parents and congregation of Sacred Heart. We are grateful to the nuns who now reside at the Felician Motherhouse in Livonia, Michigan for their generosity in sharing with us their memories.

In the next Chapter we will take a close look at how the black community reacted to the aid the missionaries provided during a period of growth leading to prosperity and then to decline.

CHAPTER FIVE
Building the Legacy

Sacred Heart parish benefited from a fortuitous confluence of people and circumstances. An energetic and forceful black Catholic community took advantage of the aid offered by thoughtful and generous religious who lived the faith. Bishop Gallagher increased the number of parishes at a time when the Church enjoyed strong support. He included the black population in the growth. Archbishop Mooney continued that support largely through collaboration with a fearless and hardworking priest, Father Thiefels. Father Thiefels, in turn, welcomed the services of dedicated Felician nuns. The nuns' Superiors, Sisters Lucille and Mansueta especially, led a valiant group of women in support of the parish and school. Sacred Heart also gained from the congregation and parents who worked tirelessly and creatively to produce a growing and vibrant community. We cannot do justice to all who contributed. We are dependent on often-meager records to try to piece together a picture of a volatile time. But the records and surviving memories give us some hint of the way these brave people took on a daunting task.

Sister Mansueta is on the right

Father Henry Thiefels, C. S. Sp.

We get a glimpse of how much Archbishop Mooney relied on Father Thiefels in a letter the Archbishop sent to Father Plunkett, who was apparently the decision-maker with regard to the participation of the Holy Ghost Fathers at St. Peter Claver and Sacred Heart.

> July 27, 1939
>
> My Dear Father Plunkett,
>
> When you kindly consented to allow Father Thiefels to be put in charge of Sacred Heart Parish in Detroit, circumstances were such as to recommend dispensing with what would ordinarily be the formalities in such a case. As I am sure you understood at the time, we were making an experiment the outcome of which was not entirely certain.

It is in no small measure due to Father Thiefels' tact, as well as Father Hoeger's cooperation, that I am able to say that the experiment has been successful and the transfer of the colored people of St. Peter Claver's Parish to Sacred Heart Parish has been effected without any inconvenience. It seems to me, therefore, it is time to ask you formally if the Holy Ghost Fathers will take charge of Sacred Heart Parish in the same way as they were responsible for St. Peter Claver's Parish. It will probably be easier for you to accept if I assure you that this arrangement will imply the gradual discontinuance of the use of St. Peter Claver as an independent parish church.

Hoping you will see your way clear to accede to my request, and thanking you most heartily for your cooperation in caring for the colored people of Detroit, I am, with every good wish,

Cordially Yours in Christ,

Archbishop Detroit

Sacred Heart Archives

From our current vantage point, we are almost amused by the circumspect way in which the letter describes an obviously delicate issue. The "circumstances" which would not allow the "traditional formalities" most assuredly would have referred to the opposition of the Germans and, likely, Italians as well who then used Sacred Heart. We learn from the use of the term "experiment" that the Archbishop must have gotten a lot of negative feedback for stepping out into uncharted territory, that is, the decidedly bold step of providing a Catholic Church home for African-Americans.

Archbishop Mooney was clearly happy with the work of Father Thiefels. He had good reason to be so happy. Father Henry Thiefels was highly influential in the years of growth. He provided the essential leadership to build the parish. He, like the nuns, had to survive on what little he could pull together from various sources. In his capacity as nominal head, he was responsible for everything concerning the church, the rectory, the convent and the school. The poverty of the parish had to be a constant source of worry for him. Yet, he persevered and brought his flock through some really tough times. While we have much evidence of the results of his efforts, we have precious little concerning his own state of mind. What that state of mind might have been can be deduced from a rather intense letter he sent to the editors of the Detroit Tribune Independent, a newspaper widely read in the black community.

December 9, 1936

Dear Mr. Editor,

With reference to your editorial in the September 5th issue of your paper entitled "Detroit's Negro Catholic school," I would like to state emphatically that St. Peter Claver Church is not opening a school under any other title except that of a Parochial School. Various papers in this city have published articles in which St. Peter Claver Parish school is called the first Negro school, school for Colored, etc., but this was done by misinformed persons and not by me nor by the Church to which I belong.

We of the Catholic faith, in spite of what individuals say to the contrary, do not draw the color line. Walk into any Catholic Church in the city or in the diocese and you will see for yourself that this is true.

St. Peter Claver Church like any other church in Detroit or elsewhere has a right to open a parochial school for its children wherein the name of God is respected and wherein its children are taught respect for parents and for country because there is a God to reward or punish.

We do not blame you or hold any ill will against you for your editorial as the local papers from which you doubtless drew your information put a false light on our undertaking. We have not opened this school as a means of proselytizing children. No one is obliged to enter this school and parents who do send their children to it may rest assured that they will be given an education equal to that given by any school in the State of Michigan. We are under state supervision, and to recapitulate, we have a parochial school first, and if the children who do come here happen to be colored – this is entirely incidental. The children who go to St. Josephat School are Polish; the children who go to San Francesco School at Brewster and Rivard Streets are Italian, etc., but this is so only because the churches are composed of these national groups. So also for us. As a matter of fact, St. Wenceslaus School at Leland

and St. Antoine is in a Bohemian Parish but had a hundred Negro children enrolled last year. At Sacred Heart School (German) at Eliot and Rivard, Negro children constituted a large percentage of the total number enrolled. And at St. Mary's School at Monroe and St. Antoine, there were many Negro children in attendance. There are many other schools throughout the city that had Negro children in attendance. If objections are sometimes raised over the admission of Negro children in Catholic schools because of lack of space, we cannot complain as these schools are private schools supported solely by the members of parishes in which they are located. If my neighbor refuses to lend me butter and eggs and to support my child, he is doing it on the same grounds as these churches are refusing at times to admit Negro children; that they must take care of their own first. It is not a question of color. It is a question of finances as 100% of the burden of these schools is borne by the parishioners. If it costs the Public School System which is supported by the taxpayers, from $80.00 to $90.00 per child to educate each of our young, how do the Catholic Schools do this without any aid, either from the State of local governments? It is because the parishioners of the parishes are willing to bear this burden.

So we, too, will care for our school. We have a right to be independent of the charity of other parishes for the education of the children of our parish and so we are opening our school for our children and for those whose parents wish their children to be entrusted to our care.

We reiterate, we bear no ill-will for your article and we thank you for permitting us to make our position known to your readers and the community we are endeavoring to serve.

Reverend Henry P. Thiefels, C. S. Sp.
Pastor: St. Peter Claver Church, R. C.

Sacred Heart Archives

This highly impassioned letter puzzles us in the extreme. From what we have been able to ascertain about the situation within the Church concerning black people, the arguments that Father Thiefels makes run directly counter to the reality. Surely he could not have believed what he was saying. We must use our understanding of the position of pastor to make any sense of it.

If we put ourselves into Father Thiefels' shoes, we can feel the pressure he was under. Several publications, including The Michigan Catholic, had referred to St. Peter Claver as a school for Negroes. The "experiment" mentioned in the letter from Archbishop Mooney probably had to do with integrating black people with white. If that experiment had any chance of succeeding, white people would have to feel welcome at St. Peter Claver. If it became common knowledge that it was for black people, white people most assuredly would have felt unwelcome. The second pressure point has to do with the need to defend the Church itself. Acknowledging that St. Peter Claver was, in fact, the first school for black people would be an open admission that the Church had collaborated with whites in the brutal act of segregation. Father Thiefels, good soldier, might have felt compelled to fall on his sword to preserve the reputation of the Church.

One other possibility exists. Father Thiefels had worked with the congregation long enough to feel a deep and abiding love for his flock. We know that he worked tirelessly to nurture the group and to increase their numbers. We can imagine that he believed his letter would defend the parishioners and parents against the likelihood of resegregation and consequent isolation. Whatever his motivations, he could not fend off the inevitable. White people abandoned the neighborhood, the parish and their Christian principles. St. Peter Claver was, indeed, a parish and school for black people.

Parishioners and Parents of Abiding Strength

Obviously, the predictions about the demise of the parish following the departure of white people were almost hilariously premature. The parishioners and parents accepted Sacred Heart as their church home and made it their own in their own way, typically creative by absolute necessity. What the doomsayers had not taken into consideration was the possibility that they could be wrong in their assessment of black people. The doomsayers were too quick to believe their own propaganda. They were too quick to pretend not to see the reality. In the Addendum to this story we have included a piece entitled, "Poetry of a Parishioner." There are two poems by one of the Sacred Heart parishioners, Cynthia Henderson, that show the creativity, the power and the insight that sustained the congregation. They indicate the patience, built on a foundation of pride that allowed the parish to persevere in the face of continuing evil.

Sacred Heart Priests

The leadership that Father Wuest, Father Kapp and Father Thiefels provided gave the parishioners and parents the safety, security and opportunity to express their creativity in building a community that met their needs. Some of the parishioners remember enough to give us a good picture of what the Sacred Heart community meant to them.

My parents came to Detroit in 1910. I was five years old. I don't know how the black Catholics began to get together. They were not happy because they could not participate in the activities of the churches. The group had enlisted the help of Father Joseph Wuest. He was a tall, kindly man as I remember him. They started a mission that began in a classroom of St. Mary's school. The room was converted into a chapel on Saturday and converted back to a classroom on Monday morning. Father Norman Dukette was a seminarian at the time.

During the next few years, the women had supper parties and held many whist parties. They did everything they could to make money. The group had to show the ability to be able to make and save a certain amount of money before the Archdiocesan Development Fund would lend a helping hand. By 1915 the group had grown somewhat and moved into St. Peter Claver Church.

There was much scrubbing and cleaning of windows, polishing of pews and getting the little church ready for the first Mass. The men, women and even the little children took part in the cleaning. The little church had been unused for some time so there was much work to be done. Every one was so happy to at last be able to go to their own church.

Father Kapp was there for years during my growing up period. The church was growing. There were bazaars, dinner parties, card parties and little plays put on by the children. Miss

Frumvilla did the training of the children. She was a sainted woman. She also played the organ for the Masses and directed the choir.

By 1940, we had outgrown the little church and moved to our present location. We will probably remain here. My mother had sung in the choir up until her last illness in 1940. I have been an active member of this church group for most of the seventy years of the existence of the black Catholic movement in Detroit.

Margaret Dean
Fourth generation Catholic
Great grandparents were slaves

This stalwart parishioner corroborates, from first-hand experience, the intensity of the founders of the parish. In her description, she named a number of parishioners. Her memory attests to the importance of the individuals who supported each other while caring for their church. They made do with what they had, and then added all of the devotion and love that continues to characterize the parish.

My grandfather's name is on a plaque at Sacred Heart. My Grandmother used to cook down in a tiny little room in the basement of the school. Father Thiefels was stern, but a good pastor. He was no nonsense. He was nonjudgmental, but clear about right and wrong.
Josephine Carter

Father Thiefels was so loveable. Everybody loved him. He was a funny guy.
Jean Hankinson Duckett

Father Thiefels taught the children to sing "Found A Peanut." He would have peanuts in his pockets and make them disappear.
Dolly Lancaster

I went to St. Peter Claver from the second grade and then to Sacred Heart. In the 40s they built the Brewster Projects. There were four priests at Sacred Heart at the time. One of them was Father Carron who was a jolly, older priest who would walk the children home from school and stop in to visit.
Lorraine Thomas

I was 12 years old when my family came to Detroit from Birmingham, Alabama. I wasn't Catholic, but I loved to read and read a story about a girl who became a nun. Two years later, I had a dream that I would become a Catholic. I began coming to Sacred Heart in 1951. I lived on 12th Street and took the bus to Sacred Heart because it felt like family. The church still had some old white people coming and some of the Germans still came back to have Masses said for their funerals.

There were five priests here at one time. Father Kirschbaum was ramrod straight and strict. When children were noisy in church, he would stop Mass and tell the parents to get the children out of there. But the people liked him. He would visit them in the hospital and he was fair.

Elfrieda Bell

I have been a member of Sacred Heart since 1985. A friend encouraged me to come. I really like the friendly atmosphere. I first came to Sacred Heart in the 1950s for a wedding. There was a German priest here and he told the people there, "You don't talk in a Catholic church." When he said that, I decided that I would not go back to that church, even for a wedding.

Gloria Gibson

When my courtship with my husband started, the teachings of Sacred Heart became evident. My husband was not Catholic and took instructions from Father Kirschbaum who was serious and passionate about our religious obligations. Like my parents before me stayed with their parents, my husband and I stayed with my parents. We had no car at the time, so we walked to Presentation Church. Father Kirschbaum, who had no car and apparently traveled by bus, came to see why we had not been to Sacred Heart. He showed his consideration by indicating that he understood and accepted our position.

Gloria Wright

Father Kirschbaum was a racist. I remember he called to Mary Frances, "That little black girl in the back."

Jean Hankinson Duckett

The picture we gain from these testimonials attests to the warmth and generosity of the culture that had been developed at Sacred Heart under the leadership of the pastors and priests. They also point out how discipline and adherence to order played an important role in providing boundaries for behavior. There is a clear tension between a culture that is warm and nurturing and one that insists on rules of behavior. Reconciling the tension is critical to understanding the legacy of Sacred Heart. We will use these notions to account for the disparate views the parishioners had of Father Martin Kirschbaum.

Father Martin Kirschbaum

Father Martin Kirschbaum evoked complex responses to his persona. Elfrieda Bell described him as "ramrod straight." He was that and more. In posture, demeanor and manner of speaking, he demonstrated what it means to be disciplined. When viewed from that perspective, one can appreciate that he asked no more of others than he asked of himself. His manner and bearing could be terrifying to the children.

> One or another of the priests would conduct our religion class from time to time. When Sister would announce that Father Kirschbaum would teach the class, the students would look at each other with fear and trepidation. Minutes before he would arrive, Sister would prepare the class. She did not have to say much more than, "Father Kirschbaum is on the way." All of us would sit up straight, fold our hands and sweat. When he entered the class, there would be no sound. I wondered at the profound effect he had on us until one incident that I can see clearly to this day. Some of the boys had been particularly rambunctious. They had not completed their taunts before Father arrived. His arrival had the usual effect until a couple of the boys in the back could no longer contain themselves. He spotted two boys who appeared to be fidgeting. He demanded that they come and kneel in front of the class facing the chalkboard as he continued the lesson. One of the kneeling boys heard a whisper behind him. The unfortunate kid forgot himself for a moment and turned to see who had dared. Father's response was swift and deadly. He smacked the kid with an open hand so hard that the poor boy went sailing across the highly polished wood floor and came up short against the wall. From that point on, no one could possibly misunderstand what it meant to pay attention when Father Kirschbaum spoke.
>
> Student

This student gave us more insight into Father's impact having served with Father Kirschbaum as altar boy at the Masses at which Father officiated. Was Father racist? The answer is lost to history. We are certain, however, that the lessons Father taught in both word and deed were lasting ones. Regardless of his motivations, the children learned obedience, the necessity for order as a precondition for learning and the value of self-discipline to achieve one's goals.

The other lesson the student suggests that one might have learned with Father Kirschbaum was that he did not allow social niceties to interfere with his determination to do the right thing. Gloria Gibson describes "the German priest" who announced to the gathering "you don't talk in a Catholic church." Any disturbance in church during his Mass was sure to get a baleful look at the very least. Any one who would dare continue the disturbance would be confronted in no uncertain terms. This willingness to be forthright and honest about the truths that one holds dear in spite of social disapproval was a valuable lesson that strengthened the students for the journey ahead of them. The emphasis that Father Kirschbaum placed on order and decorum was a hallmark of Catholic schools at the time and served Sacred Heart very well.

Sister Lucille and Sister Mansueta

Sister Lucille preceded Sister Mansueta as principal during the early growing years of the parish and school and, consequently, both were responsible for the leadership and guidance that helped to build the Sacred Heart legacy.

Permanent school building across from the church on Eliot.

I always liked Sacred Heart church. You had to be on your best behavior when Sister Mansueta came around.

JoAnn Cain

From Father Thiefels to Father Kirschbaum to Sister Lucille to Sister Mansueta, there is a constant theme of discipline and proper behavior. There can be no effective learning without discipline. The two Principals, Sisters Lucille and Mansueta, were no-nonsense proponents of discipline as a precursor to success in life. The two presided over the most productive period in the life of the Sacred Heart School. The teaching nuns assigned to the school were often relatively new to religious life and many were new to teaching. Too often, the teaching nuns were resident for only brief periods. The burden was on the Principals to provide some continuity, a strategic plan and a tactical process that would complete the mission to the black people of Sacred Heart. We have heard vivid testimony from those who attended the school which tells us that the nuns carried out their mission in admirable fashion. These testimonies are too voluminous to include in this story. Having heard these testimonies, we can only pay our own humble tribute to the work of these important leaders in the history of the parish.

The Legacy

The priests and nuns at Sacred Heart provided guidance and nurture that allowed all who took part to build a set of values. Parishioners and students and, often, the parents of the students, adopted values that provided bedrock support for life. From the records we have uncovered and from the testimonials provided by those who remember, we believe that these are the values:

Having a strong faith in the Providence of God will bring personal peace.
Relying on prayer can still anxiety.
Understanding that poverty is not the end of life can bring peace even in dire situations.
Having the ability to see clearly the sustaining power of strong values, such as accepting others, collaborating with others and helping others can contribute to planning a way through the most difficult of circumstances.
Having the ability to gain a uniquely personal form of wealth by sacrificing one's self and one's goods in service to others can help one to avoid the destructive pursuit of material wealth as an end in itself.
Cherishing the belief that following the path of Christ provides more rewards than chasing wealth and power.

Knowing that relying on the Word enables one to stand up with confidence and strength in the face of unrelenting assault by the siren song of unbridled acquisition.

This legacy of Sacred Heart held the congregation together when a changing world came close to destroying it.

CHAPTER SIX
Decline and Rejuvenation

Father Julius Zehler, C. S. Sp., took over the parish following the departure of Father Thiefels. Father Zehler enjoyed the benefits of a well-established congregation that had become sure of itself and ready to establish larger credentials. During his tenure, he welcomed to the parish a choir director, Clarence Hightower, who was to have profound impact on those credentials. During this period in Sacred Heart history, Clarence Hightower arguably became the single biggest draw for black people as well as others. He and his accompanist, Ernest Peltier, revolutionized Sacred Heart music with such force that the name of Clarence Hightower is spoken with awe, gratitude and appreciation to this day.

Ernest Peltier is on the left. Clarence Hightower is on the right.

I have been singing in the choir since I was a child. I remember singing in the loft in the 1950's. Clarence Hightower and Ernest Peltier were in charge. At that time the Mass was in Latin. There were no drums or horns and no shouting, "Amen" and "Thank you Jesus." Music was Gregorian chant, no gospel music. Mr. Hightower brought Mr. Prince, organist at Mt. Zion Baptist Church, to teach us about gospel music. Mr.

Hightower
knew classical music. He always emphasized diction.

The singing affects the church because it has touched people.
Someone may be feeling down and out and the choir's singing
can touch them to make them feel better. A person can express
himself or herself through the song. They can feel the spirit
coming through them. Some move with the beat as they feel
the spirit.

Cassandra Daniels

When I first got engaged, I brought my intended to Sacred
Heart. She did not want to be a part of it. It had fallen on
hard times. Choir rehearsals were held in the basement of
the rectory. I got married outside of Sacred Heart and that
disappointed Mr. Hightower. After a big argument with my
wife, I thought about Sacred Heart. When I drove down to the
church, the first person I met was Mr. Hightower. I have never
left again.

Stephen Tate

I remember the excellent choir Sacred Heart had when I first
came: Gerry Adams, John Blue, others. Mr. Hightower had a
variety of songs, spirituals, gospel and classical.
I miss the spirituals because they seem so healing. The
repetition used in spirituals was like a mantra. Black people
had been so oppressed. On Sunday they needed healing.
Other people seem to think gospel singing is just as healing.
Now we have Praise songs, which is an attempt to merge white
music with black spirituality. "They don't quite make it, but
praise songs is where they can all get together."

William Mims

I remember Mr. Hightower. He was a big part of the growth at
Sacred Heart. When he died, it was a big loss.

Josephine Carter

The late Clarence Hightower at work

And Ernest Peltier, just as absorbed

These views of the effect that Clarence Hightower had on the church are but a small sample of the qualities of a complex and powerful man. He "knew classical music and emphasized diction." These skills fit perfectly with the traditional church and its emphasis on meditation, devotion and excellence. After the Second Vatican Council authorized the use of "music that the people know," he introduced gospel music. That was a perfect fit for the first black Catholic congregation in the state of Michigan that was now ready to adopt a new set of credentials. Instead of relying on his own considerable skills, Mr. Hightower sought collaboration with an expert in gospel music, the organist at a major Baptist church. The result was that music and choirs at Sacred Heart became one of its defining characteristics as well as one of the cornerstones of its rebirth. In one highly talented person we again get a picture of the source of the power and influence of a remarkable church, strong devotion, emphasis on collaboration and attention to the needs of its congregation.

Elements of Decline

We had to ask ourselves, "With so many good things happening at Sacred Heart, why did it decline to the point of extinction before it recovered?" Again, the answers can be found in the enormous, even cataclysmic forces operating in the society of which the church was a part.

Sacred Heart, as an African-American parish, owed its existence to the fact that there was no other Catholic church that would tolerate the number of black people who requested admittance. St. Wenceslaus had closed rather than continue with white people in the minority. In essence, in order to ensure freedom of worship and to control its own affairs, black people had to be at Sacred Heart. This sad, but essential situation began to change in the early 1950's. The lynching and riots of the 1940's had made the Church, particularly in Rome, aware of the need for it to take a stand. The result was that schools formerly closed to black people began to open up. Students at Sacred Heart now had other options. Enough of the students left to put even more pressure on an already severely strapped parish.

This was one of the paradoxical effects of integration. As black people dispersed themselves into areas formerly reserved for white people, they lost the solidarity, the collaboration and the mutual support that had sustained them through the hard times. The power that they had generated during times of stress now began to dissipate as their burdens became lighter. Sacred Heart parish was among the losers.

A rather subtle factor in the stresses that plagued Sacred Heart had to do with the emphasis of Church teachings.

> I was in high school. Many of my classmates had left after the eighth grade to go to other schools. I remember quite distinctly my reaction to a comment made by one of the nuns in response to the brutal murder of Emmett Till in Mississippi. This 15-year-old boy from Chicago, there on a visit, had the audacity to whistle (allegedly) at a white woman. An all-white jury acquitted her husband and his accomplices. The nun, addressing the issue with the class said, "If he hadn't whistled at her, it would not have happened."
>
> Even without the wisdom of hindsight, I was aware that this was an odd position to take. I was certain that she was well intentioned. After all, the nuns had devoted their lives at Sacred Heart to producing good behavior. Obviously, whistling at a woman was considered to be boorish behavior. I marveled at her apparent inability to focus on the victim and the heinous nature of the crime. Her rules remained intact in spite of the evident need to see beyond them. Her intended message seemed to be, "Be good little Catholic boys and girls and such vicious things are not likely to happen to you." Even at my young age I could say (to myself of course) rather sarcastically, "Yeah, right."
>
> Student

Unknown to either teachers or students were the profound changes that were even then occurring in the Church and US. The rigid rules of order and the unquestioning obedience to authority were under assault by a combination of forces. Within the Sacred Heart community, students had begun to question the place of Catholic teachings in the world around them and everyone began to look more closely at their leaders, both within the Church and outside of it.

> Sacred Heart to me was a home away from home. It was safe, loving and disciplined. But, the principles they taught were not useful in the real world.
>
> Rosemarie Block Evans
>
> I liked the quietness of the Latin Mass, but I didn't understand

it. Father Stegman was rigid and would not have allowed loud singing. He didn't seem to understand black people and didn't want to be bothered by black people.

Alma Swain

I remember Father Stegman as being very stern. I did not go to the rectory when he was there.

Chalonie Livingston

My mother was in her 60s when she married again. Father Stegman didn't want to marry them because they were too old.

Lillie Brown

I remember not being allowed to go into the rectory under Father Stegman.
We could go only as far as the back door.

Cassandra Daniels

The years I spent at SH school (1947-1953) and church were enjoyable, but also extremely rewarding. I lived approximately two blocks from SH. But, every Monday through Friday, I would take the scenic route to school. My mother worked and had to escort me to the home of my relatives on Illinois street. That was eight blocks away. So, every morning, five days a week for three years, I walked sixteen blocks to Sacred Heart, which was only two, blocks away. Six days a week I attended Mass. Mass was in Latin with Father Martin Kirschbaum and numerous others saying Mass. I recall the strong smell of incense during each Mass, the ritual of kneeling, standing and sitting at each Mass and the Way of the Cross on Good Friday. I remember the meatless Fridays and weekly "Bless me Father for I have sinned."

I recall the confessionals and Midnight Mass on Christmas Eve as a joyous time. Not only because it was the eve of the birth of Our Lord, but it was also a time of great anticipation for the arrival of Santa Claus after Mass.

Mass was said in Latin at the church, but English was preached at the school. Sister Superior and numerous others pronunciated, enunciated and diagrammed the English language until Latin was a repose to hear on Sunday mornings.

Sacred Heart school brings back memories of the paraffin-waxed floors, the scent of ivory soap that always followed the nuns and the ever-presence of Mr. Hightower. I miss the monthly trips to the Eastern Market with the Sisters and my little red wagon.

I remember fondly the Teasleys, the Carters and Jaggers. But, I don't miss the stinging feeling I had after being hit by a ruler-swinging nun or the sore fingers from writing one hundred times, "I will not talk in class."

Yes. They were rewarding and enjoyable times.

Wendell Hazely

The parishioners vilify Father Stegman, but Wendell Hazely brings us back into focus. What Father Stegman intended will never be known now. In all fairness, we can conclude that Father Stegman and the practices he must have relied on in his career were quite out of place in a parish in the throes of radical change. In kindness, we might say that he must surely have been perplexed by the "strange" situation he encountered in this uniquely African-American parish. Some of the comments we have quoted reflect the increasingly common tendency at that time to observe the leaders and question their motivations. Wendell Hazely, however, captures the full essence of the impact of the traditional church. The ritual, the disciplined but nurturing nuns, even the opportunity to help, a hallmark of this poor parish, enthralled him. But the Church, the community and, indeed the United States were changing in ways that left Father Stegman in a time warp from which he apparently could not recover. What we can deduce with confidence is that he was the wrong person with the wrong plan at the wrong place and at the worst time in history for what he had to offer.

Detroit Freeways

Even as Sacred Heart was losing membership due to desegregation, another factor dealt a devastating blow to both the church and to the surrounding community. In his book, *1984*, George Orwell defined political "doublespeak" as the type of in your face lie that says one thing and means just the opposite. In a classic example of the

94

phenomenon, the Federal Housing Act of 1949, under the guise of "providing a decent home for every American," began the destruction of neighborhoods where black people had been segregated. We find it difficult to believe that this was not a conscious plan to do just what the Act did, that is, to remove black people from where they had been concentrated. "Urban Renewal" meant the removal of black people. Whole neighborhoods were destroyed. Homes were demolished. Stores were removed. The liveliest African-American business strip, Hastings Street, was ripped out. Black people who had enlivened their ghetto with imagination and grit and made it a place of mutual support and pride were dispersed to the winds. Their neighborhoods were paved over with freeways. Even in victory, white people had found a way to make black people bear the cost of change.

This blatant act of cynical politics came close to ending the Sacred Heart experiment. The number of people attending the church and school fell to a critical level. Father Stegman apparently had neither the heart nor the skills to deal with the situation.

> April 26, 1957
>
> Rt. Rev. Msgr. Carroll F. Deady, Ph.D
>
> Dear Monsignor Deady:
>
> Having conferred with you earlier about conditions here at Sacred Heart, I would like to have a final O.K. from you to discontinue our high school at the end of the present school year, if you deem it advisable. The Felician Sisters are in favor of this step since their teachers are badly needed in larger schools. Our enrollment is only sixty-two pupils. Because of this small number, and the lack of facilities, the Sisters feel they cannot afford the full number of teachers for an efficient high school. Further, most of the students live at a distance and do not belong to this parish.
>
> It seems to me that we would have better success by concentrating on and building up the grade school.
>
> Yours Very Sincerely,
>
> Jerome E. Stegman, C. S. Sp.
>
> Sacred Heart Archives

Father Stegman had to have been under severe pressure. Monsignor Deady agreed with the request and supported the decision to close the high school. We note that in Father Stegman's request, he voiced his concern that the parents of the students did not belong to the parish. He was unable or unwilling to rectify the problems. In 1965 he presided over the demise of the grade school. Sacred Heart was now without a school to serve as the foundation for the parish.

> Father Stegman was so dull. There were so few people at 8:30 Mass that he had to know you, but he was so dull my husband had all he could do not to fall asleep. Father Stegman did not go out to bring people in. We had nothing special going on here.
>
> Gloria Northcross Jenkins
>
> Father Stegman was conservative. His attitude seemed to be, "I'm the priest."
>
> Sherral Shaw Mallory
>
> When Father Stegman came, he stopped a lot of the activities like Mardi Gras and the dances. I don't think he really liked colored people. I really liked Father Zehler. He was compassionate like Jesus. We had lots of good priests. People moved out because of the freeway and because of Father Stegman. He didn't seem to want them to have a church.
>
> Elfrieda Bell

The parishioners are agreed that Father Stegman was racist. However, the term does not clarify the situation. There is a competing explanation for his behavior that relies on the situation he faced rather than his personal world-view. We surmise that he was simply overwhelmed by a set of circumstances for which he was nominally responsible, but for which he had no solutions. His parishioners were leaving, his high school was closing, and he had no resources on which to call. He might have felt abandoned both by the Archdiocese and the Felicians. His actions suggest that he was ready to close the church. He stopped the dances and the Mardi Gras probably to reduce his workload. He did not allow entry into the rectory probably to give himself a place of solace and peace. He was "dull" at Mass even though he must have known the few people who were there.

Rather than focus on Father Stegman's worldview, we want to emphasize that running a parish is a great responsibility requiring a wide variety of skills, including political acumen. If the pastor is not well-equipped or, worse yet, unwilling, then the burdens of the office can come to be seen as overwhelming, the demands on one's time and concentration more than one can bear. Racism, as a part of Father Stegman's persona, is possible, but we see inappropriate and ineffective leadership skills as far more explanatory.

Appropriate Leadership

The unique congregation at Sacred Heart needed a set of skills a great deal different from those that Father Stegman could bring to bear. Doubtless, the parishioners would say that the Hand of God began to operate to remedy this abominable situation. But, what solution would God likely prefer? That solution had to reside in the person of His representative, the pastor and leader of the parish. In retrospect, it is easy to see what kind of leader was needed. The fact is the new leader, Father Norman Thomas, brought just the right combination of skills and perceptions to enable the parishioners to solve their problems and save their parish. With clarity of hindsight, we can describe with some confidence what the new leader had to do and to be.

Even a cursory examination of history will show that the successful church meets the needs of its parishioners. The successful leader shows how the principles that govern the Church and the parish are precisely those that the people need to live fruitful lives. In effect, the leader has to show the congregation that what they need is what the Church, God's structure, offers. However, the leader must also be willing to listen, to feel the heartbeat of the parish, to understand how the eternal truths are manifest in the congregation. In this way, the leader learns where the parishioners are willing to go and rushes to get out front so that the paths of righteousness can be made clear.

Our observations of the people of Sacred Heart lead us to conclude that they took advantage of the experiment that Bishop Gallagher and Father Wuest initiated and pushed the envelope to its limits…and beyond. Those who were sent to them with love in their hearts were showered with love. Those who provided support to them while harboring vague notions of superiority were tolerated. Those who showed disdain or incompetence were expelled with comparable measures of distaste. There was no defined plan of action and no apparent collusion to guide these reactions. There was simply a devout group of seekers who were desperately in need of security and space to achieve. They succeeded in ways they, even now, would not be able to articulate with any degree of uniformity.

In the early stages, they apparently were content with strong direction provided by a confident Church that laid down rules, regulations and procedures that guaranteed Heaven, Hell or Purgatory. The priest and leader was the repository for all information and dispensations that would allow entry to the Divine. Father Thiefels and Father Kirschbaum along with their counterparts, Sister Lucille and Sister Mansueta were near perfect for the needs of the congregation. Then the world as they knew it underwent a sea change. Emmet Till, Dr. Martin Luther King, Jr., Malcolm X, the Black Panthers, H. Rap Brown and Stokely Carmichael were among those who transfixed the whole world and energized a dormant powerhouse, the African-American nation within a nation. Father Stegman was in the wrong place at the wrong time. The leadership he offered was out of date and his likely motivations insufferable.

Father Norman P. Thomas, Diocesan Priest

Father Norman P. Thomas, a diocesan priest, was appointed by John Cardinal Dearden in October of 1968 to replace the last of the Holy Ghost Fathers, Father Stegman. We are quite certain that Father

Stegman had to have been relieved to pass the reins to Father Thomas. We can imagine that even the Holy Ghost order might have been relieved to pass the baton to someone else. The Holy Ghost priests had done a remarkable job of bringing the congregation along to its then present state. They had tackled a task that was not only difficult, but exposed them to censure from their own people. The censure had to make the job that much more burdensome. While they could congratulate themselves on their successes, they probably could not see much more than loss in continuing the experiment. There was a strong need for new ideas and new approaches to supporting the congregation at Sacred Heart. Father Stegman, to the end, displayed remarkably insensitive behavior. He left twelve cents in the cash box and left, unceremoniously, a few minutes after Father Thomas arrived. He left without giving Father Thomas any information about the state of the parish.

We will let the voices of the parishioners describe the impact of the right leader at the right time in the right place and with the right plan. We will see how God provides a leader who takes his place among a people who are both ready and eager to receive his unique gifts.

My biological father was Jewish, but not by religion. He said your whole life should be centered on the church, everything: eating, partying. Your church was the sum of your life. I went to a lot of other churches, but I never saw where it was preached and practiced except here at Sacred Heart. There's no day you can come to Sacred Heart where the parking lot isn't full and there's something going on. There's nothing hardly where you can't be fed or nurtured here at Sacred Heart seven days a week. You don't have to put your religion on hold until Sunday or Wednesday. It comes into play in every part of your life. Your children, if they're interested in art, if they're interested in computers, if they need tutoring, if they go to manhood (Men of Isuthu), or Intonjane, whatever part of your life, if you want to eat, come to Sacred Heart, if you want to party, come to Sacred Heart. It's a part of my life. I never did think I would have a place like that, but that's how it is here."

Janet Moss

I am the chairman of the transportation committee. I came to a bazaar with friends in 1995. I met Father Thomas then. I saw him weeks later and he remembered my name. I really like Father's sermons. I also like the friendly people. All of this makes me feel comfortable, right at home. The parish needed drivers to bring people to church on Sunday. Groups needed transportation to go on outings. I helped work on the parish bus. Then, I went to school for diesel mechanics as a way to use my talents. Two years ago, I was put in charge.

This committee has helped to change the parish. We take seniors to things they couldn't get to and offer to do things for them. We make sure people are happy and can get where they want to go. You don't have to be a member of the parish to go on outings.

Roy Graham

I came to school here in 1959. My family had moved into the projects. We didn't have any money. I met Cheryl Shaw. At 12 years old, we went to Sacred Heart and asked to work for the tuition. We were accepted. We mended books, did the filing and cleaned the convent. My father did work too. Black people could always come here. At other schools we were always the minority. Sacred Heart was like home for being black. We had more of an identity.

I met Father Thomas at a meeting about closing Catholic schools. I remembered him. I came back to Sacred Heart in 1978. That was a time when I was having a lot of trouble. Father Thomas helped out by paying the rent, buying food and giving me work to do.

I ran into someone training women to be Eucharistic ministers. I asked Father Thomas for a recommendation and he invited me to come to be a minister at Sacred Heart. The training helped to deepen my spirituality. I had a calling to be of help even while I felt I needed help. Father Thomas gave us opportunity as women. He encourages people to do more. He shows us that we can do more. He taught me about the capacity for changing my life and moving up. Sharing the nothing that you have starts building something in you. Dorcas Bible went to nursing homes and to the burn center. Lois Glenik and Barbara Hunt went out to Phoenix prison with me to do worship service. We wouldn't have tried those things without minister training.

Cynthia Henderson

Father Thomas seems to believe that the most important people

We are willing to draw some preliminary conclusions about what began to transpire at Sacred Heart with the arrival of Father Thomas. The parish began to become acquainted with a priest who had not come to give them rules and regulations as the path to heaven. They discovered a priest who was not on a mission to make them presentable to the white culture. Here was a priest who had not come to save black people, but to demonstrate how the poor and downtrodden of whatever background can lift themselves up by living the Word. He began to show the congregation that it is not the priest who builds a church, but the parishioners. In effect, he encouraged them by his actions to take control of their lives and their church. He "walked the walk" and gave the congregants the freedom and the space to build a God and Christ centered community for which they, themselves, are responsible.

The people who offered their observations to us often gave Father Thomas high praise for what he has done and what he is doing. But, embedded in their descriptions is a common theme. Their praise for him is often subtly based on surprise and gratitude that his practices not only allowed, but also encouraged them to become much more than they thought they could be. What emerges from their descriptions is the picture of a charismatic leader who generates love and understanding and, consequently, uses the immeasurable power of the group to achieve ends that neither he nor they could achieve without collaboration, mutual respect and highly focused energy.

We are pleased to let the people speak. We are awed by their fervor.

I was going through a divorce at 27 with three young children. Father Thomas was a father figure. He said, "Come to church. You will either love it and stay or hate it and leave." I came here and I have been here ever since. I raised my kids in the church. I had a teenage boy in the streets. Father Thomas was there to help. Had it not been for Father Thomas and Pat Abner, we would not have gotten this far. The community holds me in the church. This church community helps so many lives, even outside it.

Tina Gibb

When Father Thomas gives a sermon, it's done differently than before the Second Vatican Council. The community attracts me, starting with the Pastor, because it plans and does things whether Father Thomas is there or not.

I have a cousin who was in the hospital, dying. There was another lady in the hospital. Her folks were in the waiting room and we talked. They asked about church. When I said "Sacred Heart," they said, "Oh, Father Tom's church. My sister was in the hospital dying and we didn't know who to go to so we called Sacred Heart. He didn't know us, but he came." That is traditional with Father Thomas.

I was in a class in Washington, D.C. There was a black Catholic priest there, Father Glenn Murray. I told him I was from Detroit at Sacred Heart. He said, "Hm. Why do I know that name? Oh yes, Father Norman Thomas." Everything they taught for eight days, they would say, "Oh, but Sacred Heart is already doing that."

Pat Abner

I remember rushing to church to pick up my kids. I was flying down the street when I saw the flashing lights and heard the siren. I said, "Oh my God, that's all I need."
The policeman asked, "Where are you going in such a rush?"
"I'm on my way to church."
"What church?"
"Sacred Heart."
"You mean with Father Thomas?"
"Yes."
"Well. Just slow down."

Angelia Ri'chard

I think Father Thomas is famous all over. When you say, "Sacred Heart," people say, "Father Thomas." You see him on TV a lot. He's been friends with mayors, from Coleman Young on up. This is the best and most famous Catholic church in the city."

Michael Ri'chard

"You will love it here or you will hate it." These words indicate one of the open secrets of leadership. There is no leader if there are no followers. People choose the kind of leader to whom they will respond. The congregation at Sacred Heart is self-selected. The people who remain there have found a home. Their beloved leader does the kind of things that they can appreciate. He models the behavior that they prefer. They show their appreciation and admiration by extending themselves to exhibit the same behavior that Father Thomas demonstrates. Sacred Heart is, in the minds of its parishioners, "the best and most famous Catholic church in the city." Given the respondents' observations, its reputation extends even beyond the city. One person, acting alone, could not have made that happen. What these statements from the parishioners do not make clear is that it is their own works that reflect and magnify the outstanding leadership that they enjoy.

I came in the early 1970s when there were very few people here. Father Thomas loves people and children. He said and did a lot of things that brought people in the church. He built the choir up. He kept church members involved with everything, everything imaginable. He built the ministers up, got teenagers to be ministers. He got them involved in sports, baseball teams and basketball teams. Then, there is the Gospel music...wonderful. Before, if you wanted Gospel, you had to go to a Baptist church. Then, he had the activities building built for our needs, eating, meeting and a lot of other activities. People stay here once they visit.

Father Thomas gets around. Everyone knows him. He has done so much for the community. When McDonald's wanted to build on the corner, Father Thomas got them to agree that Sacred Heart members would get first chance at the applications for employment.

Leon Smith

We do a lot for the homeless, food, haircuts, and other things. If Father Thomas asks you to do something, you do not hesitate. He treats everyone equally. He is with you 100%. He once said, "I'm short of ushers. He started calling out names. He said don't worry about the meetings, we need bodies." So, I started helping.

Walter Norwood

I remember when Father Thomas came to Sacred Heart. There was an immediate difference. He was friendly and included the members in different activities. He did not act as if he was superior. I have been a member ever since then. I worked in the religious education program teaching the First Communion class. I have also tutored children. When Father Thomas introduced the Lay Ministers Program, I entered the first class for women ministers, Ministers of Faith. Father Thomas gave most of the instructions to this group. I held the position of Senior Minister for 13 years until Mary Grace Hamilton was elected.

The Gospel music allowed by Father Thomas attracted many people to Sacred Heart. Sacred Heart has had a positive effect on my life. When I had down times, it gave me light and hope to keep going. I feel like the parishioners are my family. I try to have an effect on Sacred Heart in return. When I first became a Minister, I used to visit the sick and have a prayer service at the prison. At first this was an uncomfortable situation, but later, I got all right with it. The prisoners were very appreciative.

Chalonie Livingston Sims Hoelscher

These statements give us a good picture of how the effective leader models behavior. When the followers find it uplifting, the leader encourages them, even urges them, to do the same things. Those who have made Sacred Heart what it is have followed the lead and have taken the path. In this way, a culture has been built that now relies much less on the leader than even many of the followers recognize, although some do. Those who do recognize how they, themselves, maintain and strengthen their church, clearly say that when the inevitable happens and Father Thomas is no longer there to lead, this community of like-minded parishioners will still be there to share the load.

Innovations and Obstacles

Sacred Heart did not get to its present state without a lot of difficulty. The parish had dwindled to a very few loyalists before it began to recover. Father Thomas took the reins with a clear vision of what the church ought to be. We deliberately chose not to ask him directly about his beliefs or his vision. We doubt that he would have revealed a lot in any event. We chose, instead, to deduce his position from his actions and accomplishments. If we were to impose on him a defining moment in the history of the Catholic Church, we would settle on the Second Vatican Council. It was that Council that recognized the need for the Church to become less rigidly doctrinaire and to respond to the needs of the people. We can fantasize how this must have energized a young priest with a worldview that already focused on the needy and helpless.

When the Church authorized changes in the liturgy to accommodate the people, Sacred Heart was usually the first to make it happen.

Father Thomas exerts his influence

People respond to the message that Father Thomas offers

I remember when Father Thomas first started letting women minister, there was controversy here. There was also a red, black and green flag that hung behind the cross. That was controversial for people. Sacred Heart had to work through that. When I considered joining the Ministers program, I asked Father Thomas how should I know if I should be up on the altar? He said, "The people of the church need to be reflected up on the altar. As a white man of Lebanese extraction, I can't reflect the people. You can."

The administration, the ministry, the people run the church... not Father Thomas. He could be the Pastor and sit at his desk and keep the people disconnected from it. But, the church couldn't grow like that.

Angela Brown Wilson

When the liturgy first changed and the priest turned to face the congregation, it almost seemed like a desecration. And then the first time I heard somebody say, "Amen," I said, "What the heck is going on? This is a Catholic church. You're not supposed to do those things here." When we first started doing Gospel here, other parishes were not doing that. They would complain, "How can you do that?" Mr. Hightower was getting beaten in the head. And this was mostly from African Americans. They were the ones doing the complaining.

Pat Abner

I was baptized, confirmed and made my First Communion here. I was on the administration committee when they put the chalice in the back and the priest faced the congregation. I said, "No, no, no, put the chalice back on the altar where it belongs." Of course, I was overruled. I left and went to St. Joseph because I felt that Sacred Heart was not traditional. When the Mass was in Latin, I didn't understand it but I knew what to do. Then it was in English and I was lost. Then, all of a sudden, there was Gospel music, and it was jazzy Gospel. I was a die-hard traditionalist. I remember fighting the McDonald's. That was my mistake. That has been the best thing for the church. They've given the people jobs. They keep the area clean. They've been a good neighbor. The people here care about each other. Father Thomas has said something profound, "If the Church is to grow, it must change." He started slowly putting in Gospel music. He relaxed the dress code and the strictness.

Michael Ri'chard

> I participated in a number of demonstrations against the closing of the churches by the Archdiocese. Father Thomas said that no church had to close. People from the community could have been trained to run the churches, like our Ministers of Faith. The hierarchy figured that they had to do this.
>
> Before Sacred Heart began to feed the homeless on Sundays, I spoke out about feeling uncomfortable eating when someone else couldn't afford to buy the breakfast being served. I was surprised that a lot of people at Sacred Heart didn't want to give the homeless a free meal on Sundays.
>
> William Mims

From these statements we get the picture that the changes Father Thomas and members of the congregation introduced were strongly resisted by the people one would expect to benefit most. African-Americans strongly resisted Gospel music, the red, black and green flag and the repainting of the statues from their resemblance to white people to resembling black people. Women were the ones who strongly resisted women performing ministerial activities on the altar. Once more, this typical reaction to change reflects the fact that the Sacred Heart community culture is a product of a lot of effort over several stages of development. As changes take place, individuals must renew their decisions to remain part of the group. Sacred Heart has grown under the nurturing, but demanding leadership of Father Thomas. In a refreshing turnabout, Father Thomas would be the first to tell anyone that the "faithful few," the strong core of dedicated parishioners, have a great deal more to do with the success of Sacred Heart than his practices. Clearly, the admiration between this pastor and his flock is decidedly mutual. The result is that Sacred Heart continues to grow as the culture is strengthened and refined by the efforts of those members who choose to renew their commitment while inviting other like-minded people to come and share the values.

CHAPTER SEVEN
The Democratic Community

Father Thomas led the way in developing a community of Catholics at Sacred Heart who made the most of the opportunities that he provided and encouraged. In collaboration, they built the parish into a place many of them refer to as "home." We griots, the tellers of tales, originally took notice of this group as part of our continuing concern for, and observation of, the Black Diaspora. We have been delighted to find a place that does not solely depend on black people for its survival and prosperity. While it is true that the majority of the group is African-American, many of the people would be the first to tell you that all are welcomed and loved. In reflecting on their journey to this point, the comments that the members offer show how they marvel at themselves as well as their beloved Pastor. They realize that they "own" a church that enjoys widespread renown. They have created an environment so comfortable and accepting, that one need only visit once to feel welcome and secure.

Sacred Heart is a parish where I feel comfortable, even though I live outside the city. There are ethnic parishes around me but I feel comfortable at Sacred Heart. You know when you are home. It has nothing to do with color. You are just welcome here. I have family here and some of them are Irish. In Mississippi, the black Catholics were very closely associated with the Irish priests and nuns. They came from Ireland as missionaries.

Father Thomas makes people feel that way and others want to be part of it. People who have been anti-everything feel part of it. People can feel that they are home, they can let their hair down, not a lot of judging.

All kinds of people come...like the Polish man who jumped ship and came right to Sacred Heart. He was right from Poland and he didn't want to go to Hamtramck, he came to Sacred Heart. Sacred Heart is a port of call for all sailors. The Pope should have come here when he went to Hamtramck. He would have liked the music we have here.

Black heritage might be at the core of what happens here, but then again I say, "No" because I don't get along with all black folk. It might be some of it but it isn't the main ingredient.

Walter Joseph Williams, Jr.

I like the Mass and the way we hold hands. I have found it to be easier here to make friends and fit in than at other churches I have attended. Sacred Heart brings people together even if they don't feel like being together. It changes you. I objected to the way the Stations of the Cross had been repainted. All of the figures went from white to black. I thought other ethnic groups, such as red or yellow should be represented. This may send the message that there are only black people here. That's not so. The majority of the parishioners are black because this is an ethnic church. I stay because I like the people and their friendliness.

Diane Taylor

I considered leaving Sacred Heart once. I stayed because it was interesting being in the minority for a change. That had not been an option before. Later, I had started to get tired of hearing people say, "Oh, you must know so-and-so because she is white, too." I talked to Carol Cook who convinced me to stay by telling me, "We love you."

Bonnie Walker

I like Sacred Heart, the order of service, Father Thomas. Everybody is special to him. His sermon hits right on our needs. That is why the church is so full. There are a lot of people who live nearer to another Catholic church, but they come to Sacred Heart because it is a special place. The congregation is mixed. Nobody worries about color or about you being handicapped. When I stand with the choir and look out at the homeless in the audience, they don't just come here for the food. They could get food anywhere. If they came just for the food, they wouldn't stay until the end of the service.

Sharron Thompson

Even if Father Thomas is no longer here, in all good organizations you bury the man and continue the plan. I'd like to think that people could still be committed to the ministry of Jesus Christ, not to Father Thomas. If a pastor were appointed who was totally at odds with all of this, I would pray very hard and try to work with him. But, I would certainly have to entertain the thought, "Is there another place of worship that feeds my spirit?" There is so much good here that it should be continued.

Eric Blount

Music was certainly a great attraction for me. I heard the Sacred Heart choir sing chords that I had at home on the Thad Jones and Mel Lewis record. Then, it dawned on me some time later that the jazz music that I was seeking was rooted in the Sacred Heart choir. Jazz is a very spiritual music that came from the church and continues at Sacred Heart. Then, it dawned on me (my bulb being at about 15 watts) that there was a very special spirit about this place. It was my time to witness the spirit and I did it here. This place is truly the home of the spirit and the people are in the spirit. We have the power of God in us and with us at all times. What a place!

Just when I thought there could not be more (I was at about 5 watts by then), there was Norman P. Thomas, the Pastor and resident artist of Sacred Heart. Sacred Heart is a work of art. The Pastor works in many colors, with grace and love of his brushes. It took me a long time to see it, but Sacred Heart is brought about by the Pastor following the Spirit to build Sacred Heart and being on pretty good terms with Jesus Christ. I didn't see all of this on that first day, but I understand a lot more on my 25th anniversary.

Richard Lozon

I had begun going to the jail. Father Thomas and I had worked together on immersion summer programs for sisters wanting to respond to the Church's call to live and work among the poor. He began to introduce us to the reality of systems that bring oppression to African-Americans. After a few visits to the jail, I contacted Father Thomas who suggested that I write up a plan for ministry in the jail. He would get the funding. Gradually, the clientele grew and a number of people joined in the work.

When Sister Rita Martin finished her work as elected president of Racine Dominicans, she desired to join me. We accepted the invitation of Father Thomas to live in the convent of Sacred Heart. We joined Sister Regina Wilson there. I worked with The Public Defenders Legal Services office as prisoner advocate in support of the attorneys for the prisoners. Sister Rita knew it would be essential to structure an institution to tackle the evil so evident in the criminal justice system.

Father Thomas provided ongoing support. We found energy and faith support in the parish community, in the liturgies and in sharing cultural insights during a time of great turmoil in the city. I remember the import of social sharing after

Saturday liturgies. Mr. Hightower and Mrs. Tony Smith were important contributors to the sharing relative to black history in the Church, in the police department and other areas of the Detroit community.

I remained in the parish because never did the mutual sense of importance of faith and prayer lessen. As I moved into more work locally and nationally on racism, I always found support at Sacred Heart. I was thrilled as I watched the community grow and thrive.

Sister Joanette

Michaela Terrell gives a good picture of Sacred Heart in the early years after Father Thomas arrived.

I thought I would attempt to put down as much as I remember. I came to Sacred Heart in 1969, the year after Father Thomas did.

At Sunday Mass, the church was nearly empty, maybe about 50 people at most. There were two Masses as now, but the 8:30 was what Judy and I called the "old fogies Mass" because most of the older folks who attended. Mr. Barker was the Grand Knight of St. Peter Claver Organization, while his wife was the Grand Lady of St. Anne's Court. Periodically, the Knights and Ladies would have a Communion Sunday, as they still do, but then, the Knights wore full regalia, with plumed hats and swords. The Altar Society and Ladies Sodality also had their Communion Sundays, and mostly the ladies just wore white, but it seemed as though the Barkers kind of ruled. Mr. Barker was tall and lanky with huge hands. Mrs. Barker was plump and kind of waddled when she walked, but both of them were "in charge" no doubt.

The above Societies always had their meetings after the 8:30 Mass. Father respected their ways and didn't change the 8:30 Mass very much. Singing was congregational (still is to some degree). Mass was quite traditional, except that Father's sermons were not.

The 10:30 Mass seemed to be the Mass of the younger people. New people generally came to that Mass, probably because of the choir. I remember Maxine Adams with her high soprano (she still sings), John Blue, who had sung in Porgy and Bess, and Ruby Randall who has quite a bit of Native American in her and also had experience singing opera. She was once married to Dudley Randall, a former poet Laureate. Bob Hamilton was a member. He later got lung cancer and could hardly talk, but managed to still sing. Also in the choir were Cedric Livingston, Chalonie's father, Gwen Barnes, Cheryl Wade, and Lloyd Simpson (Tommie Terrell's father).

At Christmas Midnight Mass and some other special occasions, the choir would be joined by Gerrie Adams, who belonged to another church and also had sung on the stage. When she sang "Sweet Little Jesus Babe" and "A Land that the Righteous Call Home," tears would come to my eyes. She was a large woman and even now when I picture her with the choir, it gives me an image of heaven, like maybe, Mother Church.

Lloyd Simpson always gave the announcements and did the first two readings until Father started passing the Bible around and surprising people by asking them to do the Epistle. Lloyd was a union leader. He got all of the bulletins printed. His hobby was being a DJ and he invested in the best equipment. He did the music for all the social events, cabarets, kiddy discos, and the summer street dances held on Eliot in front of the rectory. He volunteered the union hall for parish use before we had the activities building.

After Mass, people went to the convent, later called the corner house, where Mrs. Butler always cooked breakfast. She held sway in that kitchen and allowed only one special person to help. No one else had better even poke their nose into her domain.

Four of us lived in the convent, Judy Carty (a St. Joseph sister who worked with Father), Marianne Smith (a Sister of Charity of Cleveland, a black sister very active in the group of black clergy and sisters that had started up), Regina Wilson (on leave from the Oblates), and me (a Racine Dominican). Since the parish used the convent for meetings and Sunday fellowship, we got to know the parishioners quite well. On Thanksgiving, we gave a dinner for those who would have been alone.

There were so many more. Of course, there were the alumni, although many of them had left for other parishes. There were many run-down houses all around Sacred Heart then, with lots of children. Father would gather up some of them periodically and take them to Belle Isle or somewhere. One summer we had a program for them with art and crafts and trips. Paris McCloud was one of these neighborhood children. Young people came from the Brewster projects, too, especially for the street dances.

Father managed, gradually and gently, to lead people into a greater awareness of social issues and our connectedness with all people. His liturgy gradually introduced things that would be meaningful to the people, like giving women a flower on Mother's Day, allowing children to "bring up the gifts" at the Offertory, asking for people to bring canned goods and offer those as part of the Offertory gifts, and then, very gradually, giving women a part in the Mass as Ministers of Faith. The diocese introduced a deaconate program for lay people, but it demanded a great deal of study. Father simplified things by calling men who assisted at Mass and with other services, Ministers of Service.

Mickey Terrell

There is another fascinating aspect to the Sacred Heart culture. It seems to have attracted strong-willed individuals who are seeking a collaborative community to live the Word. Lois Johnson mentioned that ex-priests and ex-nuns are welcome. We might wonder why a person in a religious order has to leave the order in order to live the Word. We have the story of one such person.

Our community (Immaculate Heart of Mary) follows the rule of St. Alphonsus and our dedication was to serve the most abandoned. I took that to heart when I was professed but I never knew what "most abandoned" meant or where they were. My mother always helped anyone and everyone who needed her, even if they did not know they were in need, so I think I just followed her rule and attitude toward people. I worked on Alexandrine with some teenagers in a storefront. The director said that when I was there the teens did not smoke pot or cuss. My provincial superior questioned me about going to this place in the evenings and told me it was not appropriate. I tried to quote the rule of St. Alphonsus to her because I was confused by her admonitions. I thought these kids were "abandoned". They worked on their homework with me, talked about trying to stay out of trouble, and they would say a prayer with me before leaving. Well, I was forbidden from returning to that place and in protest I said that if I can't go, send others more capable in my place so that these kids could have one evening a week when they would not do drugs, fight, or use profanity. This was the beginning of my questioning why I became a "nun". Then, I was arrested in Mobile with a friend of mine when all we did was attend a rally, then walk out into the street. Hundreds of us were arrested, I did not plan it, but the Bishop was upset. Some priests were arrested too and he feared that the white parishes would stop supporting the "church". Again, this was an eye opener for me.

What was happening in Mobile was wrong as far as employment practices were concerned and Jessie Jackson had come into town. My friend, Leslie Dickinson White, and I never wanted to be arrested, we just wanted to show our support. ... Those southern white cops don't play.... so that song --"Ain't gonna let nobody turn me around"... really meant something that night when we tried to leave the hall and walk out into the street. We were stopped but we refused to "turn around". My community did not say anything about it other than "who's going to pay the court costs?"

So now I am not under any "community rule." I and the friends that I have had over the years have the same attitude of just doing what needs to be done as we see fit. I don't need the community judging the circumstances for me, nor the "Church". Nuns today think more for themselves and remain faithful to the community, but I felt hampered (deeply hurt) by the random way of assigning us to our "missions". I decided that I knew how to live the dedicated life that I wanted to live without others controlling my living circumstances. I love my community and I love what I learned about life while a member, but I love my life now and I love the freedom to choose my commitments. I really follow my mother's rule - if someone needs help, help them!! Plain and simple. Opportunities are always around us.

Carole Lasker

Here is an individual who is brave enough to leave the safety and security of a large, protective organization to have the freedom to pursue the aims that that organization espouses. Carole's superior obviously had the best interests of the community as well as the nun in mind when she refused permission for a single nun to operate in an unsafe environment at night. After all, the exposure to liability costs had to be extreme. Not to belabor the point, but organizational rules and protective mechanisms often work to counter the vision and mission that the organization has adopted. You can see why we are so pleased to have found a parish, primarily composed of black people, but which welcomes all and attracts those who are most highly committed to living a life of service to those most in need in spite of costs and consequences.

Inevitably, another leader must take the place that Father Thomas has held for an extraordinarily long time. Eric Blount's comment, "You bury the man and continue the plan," is a very succinct way of showing how confident the congregation is that they will continue the good work. But, what of that next leader? We have seen how much difference appropriate skills, vision and energy can make to the life of a community. Democracy, for all of its virtues, can quickly become anarchy without a leader who brings to bear a style that fits the needs of the group. We would do well to examine more closely the kinds of things Father Thomas does that get such an intensely positive response from the members.

Father Thomas, Father Cunningham, Father Kosnik and Father Finnigan along with Bishop Gumbleton all went to Sacred Heart Seminary and all got a reputation for being renegades. "Renegade" meant it was not the traditional Catholic Church approach. We were in Washington, D. C. when they excommunicated the black priest who was doing the same things these guys were doing.

Gale Northcross
Gloria Northcross Jenkins

Father Thomas also brought a following with him when he came here. He was an activist, a Civil Rights bus rider and had been in the movement for a long time. He encourages us to get involved. Sometimes, I think he gets a little disgusted with us because we have such a poor showing. Then we had the change from Latin to English, the altar turned around, the removal of the communion rail and the introduction of ethnic music and art. Mr. Hightower and Mr. Peltier supported that last. Then we had collaborations with Shiloh and some other Baptist churches.

Karoy Brooks

I asked Father Thomas, "How do you remember everybody's

name?" He answered, "I want to."

Father Thomas wants us to be self-sufficient. He wants to know that we will keep going when he is no longer here. One of the reasons I remain here is that we feel free to grow, to take part, to take responsibility. I can't see it ending because we have too many strong people who have grown and developed in this environment and know how to make things happen.

Lois Johnson

Out of the wilderness stepped the leadership to help those who did not know how to do. I have seen Father Thomas take his tee shirt and give it to someone.

Lewis Blount

Father Thomas has a lot to do with making this a family. He stands up for what he believes in, in spite of what the Church might say.

Fred Watkins

Father Thomas breaks the rules. He welcomes misfits... divorcees, people on the run, people who cannot learn the catechism. He faces the music at the Archdiocese all alone and still gets his way. He is highly insightful. He makes you aware of yourself without putting you down. The stories we can tell about him are wonderful. For example:

A person working with him in the rectory wanted an air conditioner. That would have benefited both of them. He wouldn't have it. He said, "None of the houses in the neighborhood have it, so I won't either. However, he scrounged in the attic to get an ancient fan for the other person. It worked.

One of the misfits he welcomed stole a purse from his assistant. Father Thomas went to the theater where he heard the thief had gone. He talked her into showing him where she had thrown the purse in a field.

A group of female thugs offered to clean his clock. He went to talk to them. They ended up in church at the services.

Mickey Terrell
Lawrence Terrell
Pat Crispell
Carole Lasker

A new leader will be hard pressed to provide even a close resemblance to the qualities that Father Thomas brings to the community. That need not be a death knell for the group if the new person brings the one essential ingredient, that is, a vision based on the needs of the people versus the needs of the organization, the larger Church. Such a position is not as easy as it might seem at first blush.

Father Thomas has taken some bold steps to nurture and protect his flock. He has taken even bolder steps to support his vows. His actions have, at times, brought him censure from the Church. One of his actions, in particular, gives compelling evidence of the too frequent conflict between organizational ends and spiritual ends.

Father Thomas took a very visible lead in opposing the Archdiocese on its decision to close a number of churches in Detroit. Archbishop Szoka had said that the flight of whites out of the city to the suburbs meant that the Archdiocese could no longer afford to keep the city churches open. The city churches were old and the cost of maintaining them was rising. Another factor was that there was a shortage of priests to minister to the churches. He ordered that 30 churches close and 25 others work to improve their status to avoid the same fate.

At a symposium of clerics convened to discuss options for the future, the clerics agreed that Detroit had to close some churches, but the manner in which the closings had been done was objectionable.

Father Thomas was at the forefront, leading protests and organizing defiance of the orders to close. Paradoxically, Sacred Heart could have been the net beneficiary of the orders since some black people might have chosen to migrate to Sacred Heart when they were forced out of their churches. As a large and growing parish, Sacred Heart was, perhaps, insulated from the threat of closure. This benefit did not deter the indomitable priest. His argument, in essence, was that the decision to close churches in the inner city was a blatant example of the attitude of the Church toward black people. Clearly, this openly stated position had to have put him at odds with those decision makers who were also his nominal superiors.

Baldly stated, here is the Church hierarchy on one side looking at the balance sheet. On the other side is a parish priest who has devoted his life to serving the poor and outcast openly questioning its decisions. There could not be a clearer case for choosing sides. The Church had the opportunity to examine its mission, vision and values and put to itself some hard questions. Was it to continue its dependence on and consequent subservience to its white membership? Or, would it trust in God's Providence and stay true to its stated beliefs? We know the answer. The churches closed and its lone priest shut out of the inner circle. The Pope visited Hamtramck, not Sacred Heart.

The Legacy Bears Fruit

The Sacred Heart Legacy has been preserved and nurtured so that it has a good chance of surviving Father Thomas' tenure as Pastor. Often called "The Good Shepherd," he will leave a flock capable of supporting themselves with a minimum of aid from the next enlightened and visionary priest. The parish is already managing to provide itself with the services it needs to keep its members safe in the family. The groups that they have formed and the leadership positions they have taken on attest to the firm grounding in the Word that they have absorbed. In the final analysis, it is the people of the congregation who pour the spirit and energy into the initiatives and make them their own. We understand that the parish is alive with activity even among those who are not formally associated with a named committee.

A Powerful Parish

While the parishioners are exceedingly generous in their praise for those of the religious community who came in love to support their efforts, many of the religious offer generous praise in return. The Felician nuns have said how much they gained from an association with these remarkable people. They had little difficulty in disciplining the children; the parents took it upon themselves to support the nuns fully. Father Thomas offers many examples of how the strong people in the congregation start and even demand many of the initiatives for which he subsequently receives credit. He offers the following examples.

> When the membership in the church declined, there was a core of very powerful people who knew precisely what they wanted to do to maintain and grow the church. They, themselves, supply the energy, commitment and ideas. They maintain the physical structures. They provided the funds to build the annex and its two additions. When I arrived, the church needed painting. The people did it. The people welcomed the Felician sisters, of course, but their efforts made the nuns successful in their work. The parish does not depend on one person.
>
> Father Norman P. Thomas

In light of these comments from Father Thomas, we looked once again at the comments offered by members of the congregation. We are struck by the fact that the member comments say little about the things they, themselves have done to benefit the church. We believe this to be a tribute to their unconscious, but very effective self-reliance. They are clearly grateful for the support they obtain from their beloved pastor. They do not reflect on the blood, sweat and tears that they and their ancestors supplied to make the church and the community what it is. They use stirring words to deflect attention from their own incredible journey, "This far by the grace of God." These words attest to their phenomenal survival, but also acknowledge the journey yet to come. They know that their work is not finished. We are humbled by the knowledge that this group will, indeed, soldier on.

We are mindful of the picture we have of early Christian communities. The Sacred Heart community has survived some very difficult times. It now prospers in a period of peace and tranquility. Its members might have forgotten, or choose not to reflect on, the troubles that brought them together. But, its success has depended on patience, perseverance and a steadfast reliance on the Word of God. The early Christians were not centrally organized. They could not rely on monetary support from a large bureaucracy designed to make missionary work less harrowing. Others who, at the very least, did not wish them well beset them on all sides. There were some non-Christians who actively sought to harm them. What they had was a strong belief in the Word and power of Christ. They devoted themselves to living a life based on faith and love. How like early Christians is this Sacred Heart community.

The Story Not Yet Told

We are convinced that Sacred Heart has done something quite close to miraculous. Its members started with virtually nothing and can now claim a great heritage and wide acclaim. It has grown into one of the most prominent African-American parishes in Detroit with a distinguished history. We have only begun to explore the outcomes of this epic journey. We have examined only the events, methods and people who contributed to an uplifting story. Were we to trace the impact on the lives of the individuals who lived the story and used the values and philosophies they acquired at Sacred Heart, we would have to produce an unpredictable number of pages of history. We will leave that task for another time. We will, instead, use the Epilogue to capture, for ourselves, the lessons we have learnd from an examination of this historic congregation

EPILOGUE
Meditations of the Griots

We "tellers of tales" have been privileged to recount the journey of an intrepid band of seekers. Their courage and resourcefulness have presented us with an inspiring saga. What is most noteworthy is the fact that, having suffered grievous wrongs at the hands of both the white population and the Church which they so dutifully served, the parishioners did not let that stop them from welcoming everyone to join them, including white people, and remaining true to the tenets of a Church which often acted counter to its own teachings. This fact alone would be truly amazing unless we remind ourselves that the parish survived and prospered by following God's Word. These steadfast believers subjected themselves to Church teachings to such an extent that they forced the Church to walk the talk. They made themselves a modern example of an early Christian community so unmistakably that the Church could not ignore the irony of having become a large bureaucracy that once again denied its true adherents the right to worship in its edifices.

God did, in fact, provide the necessary help at the time that it was most essential and could have greatest effect. Holy Ghost priests, Felician nuns, Bishop Gallagher, Father Wuest, Father Thiefels, Father Hoeger, Cardinal Mooney, Father Thomas, Sister Lucille, Sister Mansueta, Sister James, Sister Bernardine, Sister Humilitas, all are names which will live in the memory of those who benefited from their support and love in time of desperate need. The sacrifices that these people made on behalf of a brutally misused populace was proof enough that God operates in His own time in ways which remain inscrutable. We have no doubt that these religious took their vows seriously.

Some of those who came to serve the black Catholics expected that the results of poverty and unremitting persecution would have produced a debased and broken community that needed the services of missionaries. What they found, often to their delight, was a highly resourceful and self-reliant community composed of several levels of a thriving society. Yes, there were difficulties in both housing and

125

resources that, at times, tested the resolve of those who would serve. The courage, fortitude and strength of these religious in the service of God in spite of their travails will be worthy of praise to the end of time. Almost all of the helpers were white people. Some of them had to endure the disdain and rejection of their own people who had no way of comprehending how anyone could ally themselves with the Negroes that the majority of white people so heartily despised. To their credit, there were also those among their religious colleagues who came close to envying the opportunity of the missionaries to work among a noble and enduring people.

Challenges Ahead

Our prediction is that there are perilous times ahead for the Sacred Heart community.

In telling the beautiful tale of how the parish survived and reached a measure of prosperity, we were impressed with their disregard for the trappings of wealth and the pseudo-security of power. They and their leaders followed Christ's example of trusting in God to provide while they built a community devoted to serving the needs of those who could not contribute. Many of the parishioners have mentioned how surprised and pleased they are that Father Thomas does not beg for money. They are even more pleased that he accounts for all that he receives. We do not know if they have prepared themselves for the threat of closure.

We are fearful. Here is a community to which those in need find their way unerringly. A Polish sailor jumps ship. He does not go to Hamtramck. He heads for Sacred Heart. This story reminds us of another that we heard about a wildlife sanctuary and hospital on the coast of California. The researchers and medical personnel received a gull with a broken wing. Since the bird could not fly, they wondered how it got there. They retraced the obvious path of the gull. Retracing the path was easy. The broken wing had to be dragged along. The researchers followed the path for some two or more miles along the sandy beach. How did the gull know that it would find help there? What gave it the strength and courage to drag its wing for such a distance? There are certainly no answers to these questions. We hope the story is true for it parallels the story of Sacred Heart. Those in greatest need know there is a place where caregivers worship God. The hungry go there even though there are other places to eat. There is something at Sacred Heart that feeds more than the body. We are fearful that if the parish does not prepare itself, this place of refuge and care might not survive the next time of trouble.

What will the congregation do to ensure that its culture of caring continues?

Here is a community in which all manner of people are welcomed and loved. One of the parishioners, Roy Hoelscher, tells the story of a Viet Nam war protester who tried to obtain status as a conscientious objector.

To avoid being brought to trial, the protester fled from Chicago to Detroit looking for "sanctuary." The FBI was hunting him. By law in many countries, churches can be used as places of protection from government law enforcement. I was asked to find a church and pastor willing to help. Most of the pastors I contacted strongly agreed with the idea, but were afraid to commit to such a strong political stand because of their congregation's potential disapproval. Someone suggested I call the new, young pastor of Sacred Heart Church who had a reputation for being "very approachable, open, liberal and against the Vietnam War." When I asked Father Thomas if he would consider helping, he paused only briefly and replied, "Well, I guess that's what sanctuaries are for – to offer worship to God and to provide safety for His people who are wrongfully pursued."

Father housed the protester in the church and locked the door. A radio station, CKLW, was paying $1000.00 for the best story of the week. To publicize the strong anti-government position of the protester and to get the reward, someone let the media and the FBI know where the protester was hiding. The FBI arrived, cut the chains on the church door and removed the protester. The radio station paid the $1000.00, those who wanted the publicity got it and Sacred Heart cemented its reputation as a church for the people.

Roy Hoelscher

This incident illustrates a fundamental way of life in the parish. The parish is eager to welcome ex-nuns, ex-priests, divorcees, the twice married, and the ex-communicated. The parish also welcomes gays and lesbians who have been under severe attack, mainly from people who trumpet their supposed Christianity. The congregation welcomes all who want to share in their culture of walking the path that the Church espouses, the path of Christ. White people have joined in collaboration to work side-by-side in the mission that Sacred Heart has adopted. We have not seen evidence that other racial and ethnic groups have joined. As one of the white members pointed out, the emphasis on black cultural art and artifacts could very well deter members of other groups. If that is so, then we wonder if the black majority will reconsider.

We know that black people are hard pressed to find places where their leadership and skills are welcomed. The one place where they can assume leadership positions is among other black people. If they make conscious efforts to include members from other ethnic groups, will black people be shut out of leadership positions once again? This is an issue that requires more than a casual response.

Our hope for Sacred Heart is that the members continue to focus on collaboration with like-minded people of whatever origin. We hope that the experiences of the last 100 years will have brought home the message that without collaboration, the struggles of black people will be that much more difficult.

Will the congregation accept the challenge of including artwork representative of red, yellow, brown and white people to show welcome?

Cultural Obstacles

We have been deeply affected by our examination of this congregation. We have learned a great deal that will aid us in our continuing efforts to tell the tales of the Black Diaspora. The challenges we have posed for the congregation stem from our fervent prayer that the members recognize and appreciate what a unique opportunity they have built for themselves. Their forebears accomplished works of wonder. The parish would do itself a disservice if it does not capitalize on the heritage. By reflecting on their history they will see that they can intensify their impact on others by demonstrating, consciously, what it means to live according to the Word. We would venture to say that the legacy that the current members of the parish enjoy could very well dissipate if they do not honor it by concerted action. We hope we do not overstep our bounds by enjoining them to move ahead vigorously to take advantage of an illustrious past. The results they can achieve are sorely needed. The obstacles they face, however, are truly daunting.

The greatest obstacle is the pervasive culture of greed that permeates this nation. We are dismayed at the corrupting influences of wealth and power. However, we remain prayerful that wealth and power, in the hands of those who live by the Word, can provide a viable alternative to the callous and casual cruelties commonly visited on the poor and needy by the wealthy. To say that another way, we are not opposed to wealth as such. People need to reach a level of comfort at which the basics are not in doubt. A society must have some level of disposable wealth to sustain its artists and philosophers as well as to protect those who are unable to provide for themselves. Our quarrel is with those who continue to gather and hoard wealth to the detriment of the community. The lengths to which people will go to acquire wealth and to use it in utter disregard for those who do not have it sicken us.

How does one live a life of charity and frugality when constantly bombarded by messages of excess? How does one continue to believe Christ's words that "the meek shall inherit the earth?" That is the central challenge and obstacle facing the members of Sacred Heart. If they consciously set out to demonstrate the path, they will continue a remarkable journey. If they are successful in demonstrating the good life that does not depend on greed, obscene luxury and callous rapaciousness, they are certain to eclipse the legacy their predecessors bequeathed.

The power holders are certain to resist anyone who attempts to counter their practices or even to suggest another way to live. The

Sacred Heart congregation has demonstrated historically, albeit unconsciously, that one need not resist the power holders, one need only to ignore them. The rich and powerful can sustain themselves only by exploiting those who want to gain a share of the wealth. Those who desire the lifestyles of the rich and famous are easily seduced into doing anything that the power holders demand. The truly distressing aspect of this adoration of the rich is that even people of color who have suffered greatly are too willing to adopt the façade and trappings of power and use these to lord it over the less endowed members of their own families. The counter to this sorry state is to withhold obeisance to those who flaunt their wealth and use it to debase others. Those who know when enough is enough will not blindly sacrifice their integrity and humanity in the unceasing quest for more. They will not "go along to get along."

The religious and parishioners of Sacred Heart have shown that those who do not fear poverty, those who practice charity and those who practice obedience to the Word can fill their lives with riches untold, riches that are often invisible to the uninformed. One does not have to join the increasingly bitter battles for scarce resources. One need only reduce one's own desires and look diligently for ways to provide help to others. But such a path is not one to be taken lightly and certainly not one to be taken by the faint-hearted. The experiences of the Sacred Heart congregation attest to that. The blind faith that the current leaders of the US require is sure to lead to more of the disasters currently facing this once-great nation. The very practical faith that the Sacred Heart congregation has adopted can lead to an antidote for a confused and dangerous world.

The Greatest Challenge of All

Black people have long considered themselves to be victims of the unrelenting oppression of white people. The most disinterested observer of history will conclude that black skin and its accompanying physical characteristics is only one of numerous markers by reason of which one people will decide to, or carelessly allow the mechanisms to, oppress another. For example, the Jews have vowed never to forget the Holocaust. They erect one monument or program after another until the Germans can no longer abide the thought. The Armenians, with markedly less power and influence, are hard pressed to find ways to remind the world of the attempted genocide by the Turks. Muslims are under current assault by people who trumpet their Christianity even though those same people scrupulously avoid using the term "Crusade," a word freighted with historical import. The poor have no voice to complain about the incessant, absent minded cruelties of the rich. Virtually every group that can distinguish itself as a group can tell tales of oppression by some relevant, more powerful, other. What are we to make of this litany of oppression as it relates to Sacred Heart and its future?

Sacred Heart can promote this statement, "We are all one people."

Earth is the only vessel in the universe of which we are aware that supports living things. People of whatever variety are solely capable of preserving, or preventing the destruction of, our vessel and its life forms.

The members of the Sacred Heart parish can relax and enjoy the benefits of its heritage, the benefits of the heroic struggles of the people who laid down a remarkable history. The members can relax and go on as if prejudice and cruelty, greed and avarice, will bypass a worthy congregation, blessed by God Himself.

Alternatively, the parish can renew its strivings as the first Catholic parish in Michigan, the US, and the world, to build an enduring place of refuge for all living things. The parish can use its remarkable history as a compass on a rough road to chart a path toward a different world. That path can only be followed by those who choose to collaborate to live the Word without regard to artificial differences or surfeits of wealth.

Such a parish would not be the "first black parish in the State of Michigan." The term "black" would no longer be relevant, only a hindrance.

Such a parish would not be devoted to making its members rich. Riches and its accompanying power can only make the compass unreadable.

Sacred Heart has come this far by faith. That same faith can propel its membership to a future that only God can see.

We pray that this illustrious past be prologue to a commendable future and this worthy parish take up a great challenge.

Moving On

We hope to continue our quest to preserve the stories coming out of the Sacred Heart Legacy. We have drawn strong and most certainly provocative conclusions from our examination of the congregation, their church, the religious who served them and their community. We sincerely pray that this record of our findings will somehow repay the parish and its leader for giving us the honor of the telling.

John Lynch

Deo Gratias.

ADDENDUM

FELICIAN SISTERS OF SACRED HEART MISSIONARIES

Memories of the Missionaries

The following is a full report on the interviews taken with the surviving Felician Sisters who ministered to Sacred Heart over the school years from 1938 to 1965. The interviews were done in October of 2004.

> We had 100% cooperation from the parents.
> All we had to do was call and the mother would say, "I will be there in 20 minutes."
>
> Sister Arthur
>
> The children were polite, attentive and intelligent, obedient and happy. (There was general laughter at "obedient.") At that time it was easy.
> I enjoyed the singing of Clarence Hightower.
> It was my first experience. It was wonderful.
>
> Sister Leonette
>
> Sister Lucille always had the front door locked because of the area that we were in.
> Whenever the ladies would have something going on in the church, they made sure that we got some of that real good food.
>
> Sister Eleanor Marie
>
> Spent my first three years at SH
> It was a very strange beginning being over there, but I really enjoyed it.
> When we had accreditation, I was scared to death. What are my children going to do?
> The inspector thought the children did well in their presentation on the virgin birth.
> Then the children sang for him and they could sing beautifully.
> I never thought of these children being black or white. They were children.
>
> Sister Estelle
>
> I was in my first year of teaching.
>
> What am I going to do in this strange place? I had no idea.
> When I first entered the class, I got some impression that there was connection to St. Peter Claver. I don't know what it was

and I was too shy to ask.

My students (in a combined 6, 7 and 8) were the most active in the school.

The students were bright and intelligent. Other students who could lead or dramatize what was to be done led many of the projects.

Much of the work was done to some type of music.

There was only one white boy left in the whole group. He was very active and we didn't discriminate. We didn't recognize colors. We worked as a group and we were very happy as a group.

In June the riots broke out.

The militia came in at midnight. That impressed me. That was the first time that I realized that I was in a neighborhood that was different.

I realized this was a poor neighborhood and our mission was to help the people we were working with.

The phone began to ring. People called and said, "Sisters, if you have any trouble, just let us know. We are going to be there. We will supply you with food and whatever else you need."

Sister Fidelis

I was at Sacred Heart from 1946 to 1950 teaching seniors.

I went to the chapel and prayed, "Dear Lord, I will love them all, but I am so afraid to go. You know what is happening in Detroit and all over."

The sisters would walk outside in pairs.

When the children would see us, they would say, "Here come the Gods."

We would offer to let them touch the cincture and to kiss the crucifix.

When I entered the class, I said, "How will I ever remember their names? There are so many of them and they all look so much alike to me."

It took about a month and I knew them all. Everybody was different. No one was the same.

I came with a wonderful attitude. I am going to treat them as I treat everybody else.

Our Mistress said the same thing to us. "Don't think of them as people who are different than us. They are all children on God."

We produced an operetta. Their voices were so deep and so strong. They put so much emotion into their singing. I was amazed. I couldn't believe that someone could sing so beautifully as these high school students.

Sister Stephanie

I did my practice teaching in 1942 at Sacred Heart. I had the 4th grade. I loved every moment that I spent there. When we were sent from Presentation Jr. College, Sr. Annunciata told us, "Wherever you go, every little boy and girl is your brother and sister." We all adopted that feeling, that we accept them. I wouldn't do something that I wouldn't do to my own little brothers.

It was an honor to be at Sacred Heart. We were not given a salary. We worked for charity.

The ladies and knights of St. Peter Claver were so good to us. They would have a shower for the nuns once or twice a year. They were most charitable.

Thaddeus Jones, one of the students, came in with a branch from a cotton plant. I had never seen one before. It was so educational for me and for the class.

Father Thiefels was so good to those kids. Each of the kids was asked to make an altar in honor of Our Lady. Father Thiefels thought the altars were so beautiful he wanted to take pictures of the altars and their creators. The children were just posing and Father was taking the pictures. Later I asked, "Did you ever have those pictures developed?" He said, "Sister, I can't afford film. The kids were thrilled to be recognized as an outstanding group. That was the reward. They don't look for any more. They were pleased and happy that they did something in honor of Our Lady."

When the kids would see Fr. Carron on the street, they would call him God.

There was a poor box in the church. Fr. Thiefels realized that there was money missing from the box. He found out that Fr. Carron was taking money from the box to provide ice cream for the nuns. Fr. Thiefels admonished him and told him that the ice cream would be provided without taking money from the poor box. They were so good to us.

I was probably more enriched by those little children than they were from me.

Father Carron went into the class and was reprimanding them

for something. They all began to sing, "Oh, what could my Jesus do more?"

He came out and said, "Sister, what is wrong with those kids?"

I answered, "They are such a sensitive group of kids and they know I love that song. So that made it all right."

I was always grateful to the community for giving me the opportunity to work at Sacred Heart.

Sister Bertha

I was at Sacred Heart for a total of seven years in three intervals.

Late 1940s and late 1950's. Then late 1960's just before it closed.

I enjoyed every time that I was there.

The first time I had the 4th grade. I had James Lynch, Joyce Holder and then Betty Deramus in the seventh grade.

I had difficulty with the songs because they were in Latin. But, the children did very well. They learned so fast.

I also trained the altar boys to sing for Midnight Mass. Of course it was difficult because they were near the altar and I was up in the balcony with the organ. But, we did it.

When we would have a play, we did not have enough room on the third floor for the stage, so we went to the Brewster Project auditorium. We really had a big crowd.

In the 7th grade, Betty Deramus was such a bright girl. She wrote a letter to the Detroit Times and won the award for best article.

The last time I was there, they were ready to close the school, so that was a hard time.

The first time I was there, we didn't have a car. Nobody drove. So the Holy Ghost Fathers allowed us to drive, so I was the first to drive a parish car. We would drive to go shopping and to go to meetings at the Motherhouse.

Sister Bernardine

I am not sure of the year that I was there. It was either '46 – '47 or '47 – '48.

The children were very kind and courteous. When I went to St. Stanislaus, I would tell them, you are not one bit like the students I had at SH.

I taught Algebra, Geometry, and English.

It was a mission school and the students knew that. We came to give ourselves to them. They showed their appreciation for that.

When I went to the hospital for surgery, the only student who came to see me was from Sacred Heart. He was the school

president. That's how kind they were.
("Mission" to you means that you took no salary.) Yes.
It started with Sister Pulcheria and Sister Angelica.
It was in 1936. My mother sent me a goose for Thanksgiving
and I remember walking over to the sisters and giving the goose
to them. Here I had this goose and they had so little. That was
my mission, my first year in the academy.
That year, the firemen came over to donate their services to
paint and fix up the house.
At the time we used to get very generous donations.
They brought in many things from the market.
We never had any wants over there.
(Were you in dire straits prior to the firemen?) No.
There were things we could live without. But, we were not in
dire poverty.
The women would have a show and all of these elegant ladies
would come and spend the evening with us. We would sit and
talk and visit. It was like one big family. They would all bring
some food products and when they left we would have enough
to last us for a year.

At one point, the FBI called out a sixth grader. Her grandmother
had her peddling dope. She never returned to school.
Sister Anthony, the Principal, was so broken-hearted. "Why
would that have to happen to our school?"
Other than that, the students were marvelous.
I went on to teach at other high schools. To me, nothing was
comparable to SH.

(Were the majority of children Catholic?) No, out of 50, there
were 15 Catholics.

                                                    Sister Harold

I entered the convent in 1946.
First, I was a Postulant then a Novice.
I took my first vows in 1949.
I was at Sacred Heart from 1949 to 1951.

My first year of teaching was at Sacred Heart. A young kid of
21. I was so excited. Then, I found out that teaching is not so
easy. I had 57 kids the first year and I had nothing. But, Sister
Gastolda sat with me and helped me.

Fathers Zehler, Dooley and Kirschbaum were there.
Bishop Kiwanuka came. He had such a humble mitre on. It

141

looked so bad. Sister Lucille said, "We have to do something."
They bought gold metallic material to adorn the mitre. Even
though I did not know how to sew, they said I had to put in a
couple of stitches so that I could have a part of it. They showed
me how to put in the stitches.
There was an uprising. The people called and said, "Don't
worry sister, we will not let anything happen."
I went out back to burn some branches. A man came over
and said, "Mother, I will take care of that." The IHM's had
preceded us and they were called "mother."
When I met Father Thiefels years later, he said, "Oh, a Felician
Sister. I will always be grateful to Sister Pulcheria and Sister
Angelica for allowing your order to come and help me."
Many times, our community has done so much and we just
don't get that recognition.
We are called to work with the poor and the marginalized.
I was very happy in my work. I felt that I was really doing
mission work. "Mission" is ministering. I am doing God's
work.

[Sister Harold interjects at this point. "During the riots, the
people were so kind and generous. They waited at the bus stop
and walked the sisters home so that nothing would happen to
them."]

I recall walking to another parish and a child touched me.
My companion said, "They probably think it is good luck or
something."

Another time we were walking and one child said to another,
"Look at them ladies. Them's church ladies." I said, at least
they don't think we are devils or something.

Sister Dolores Ann

I spent one beautiful year at SH. I had first and second grades,
then a third grade was added.
I didn't have any trouble relating to them. I fell in love with
them right away.
My mother and dad came to visit. My dad had an aversion to
the Negroes. My mother always accepted everybody.
I said, "Dad, I love these children. They are God's children. I
wouldn't trade this job for anything in the world."

[Were they afraid for you? No answer].
I called a set of twins over to sing for Mom and Dad. My Dad

just looked skeptically at them. My mother was just full of smiles. They began to sing the songs I had taught them. I looked at Dad and pretty soon I saw tears coming down his cheek. He fell in love with these children. They came twice after that. My mother made a set of pink pinafores for the little girls. They were from a very poor class of family. They gave my mother a big hug that they remembered them.

I had two groups of children. The poorest were from the Hastings area. We had a busload coming from 7-mile rd and they were a more affluent type of children.

The poor ones came with lunch boxes...hard bread. The rich kids came with real good sandwiches, fruit, and candy.

The poor kids just looked at them.

The rich kids would throw out half of their sandwich into the basket.

One time I saw a child go to the basket in the corner. He would pick out the half-sandwich and put it into his pocket. No one else saw him. I later saw the sandwich sticking out of his pocket as I passed behind him.

Another little boy asked to help me after school. There were some left over milk cartons from the children who had not been in school to take them. He asked me, "Sustah, can ah haves one a dem's?"

I asked him, "Don't you have any milk at home?" "No, Sustah."

"What did you have for breakfast?" "Gruel."

We found out that it was the worst taste you could imagine... like dead fish.

I asked, "What do you put in the gruel?" He said, "Watah."

I asked, "What did you have for lunch?" He said, "Gruel."

He had the same thing for three meals.

I came back to Sister Anthony, the Principal, and asked permission to go to my friends at St. Stan's and ask for clothes for the kids.

They brought boxes full of good clothes that their children had outgrown.

That mother was so grateful.

Two of us went to see the home.

There was one mattress on the floor. No blanket or cover. Four children had to sleep there. The windows were barred with boards. It was cold and there was no heat.

One of the sisters was a social worker. She got in touch with the agency. They received a furnace. The windows were replaced. They got furniture. We gave them a lot of the used clothes. The mother cried she was so grateful.

I remember the students were so active and energetic and they had the most wonderful rhythm. Their attitude was so good.
A bridal shop was closing and the owner called and asked if we could use the bridal gowns that had to be disposed of. We accepted them and dressed the girls in these gowns for the 13-hour devotion services. When the services were done, Sister Edna told the mothers, "You can keep these dresses."
The mothers were so grateful. They never had clothes like that before.

One of the sisters and I had occasion go to Kresge's to do Christmas shopping. The store was full of people. I heard someone calling me, "Sister Audrey, Sister Audrey."
A big, tall Negro boy came up to us and said, "How's come dem left Sacred Heart for? We still love you."
When I was told to go to Sacred Heart, I was told, "Accept these children. Relate to them. Show them that you accept them." I was told, "I know that Jesus needs you there."
I went with that attitude. If Jesus needs me there, I am ready.
I had one day to pack up and go.
I accepted these children. I had the most wonderful, wonderful year with them.
Of the fifty-three years of teaching, that year stands out as the most beautiful of teaching.

I taught quite a bit of singing and dancing at the school. We had the play "Hansel and Gretel."
Sister Bernetta was there and she taught the dancing. She said, "I taught the children well."
I said, "As jivey as these kids are, I don't know if they will remember your steps, they will put in their own."
Oh, beautiful voices. You'd never have to teach a different voice. They would just harmonize. They would pick it up right there.

Father Stegman came over and said, "Sisters, I wish I could compensate you for coming over to teach for us. Take a guess how much we collect at Mass."
We guessed, 500, 700, 300. He said, "No. The maximum was $15.00."

Any donations we got, we shared with Father.
God provided for us.

[Would you comment on the fact that black people brought their children to the nuns because of the nuns' reputation for providing excellent discipline along with the education?]

I was there in 1942. All of the children were checked before they went into the classroom. For some reason or other, they carried pocketknives.
What happened prior to that year, I don't know.

[The other nuns chimed in, "That didn't happen during my time. The parents were very cooperative. If I had a problem, I would call the parents and they corrected the problem. They knew that the children would get a good education so they cooperated.]

Do you remember how we would keep the floor shined?
[General laughter]. Wax paper.

I had a vocation in my class.
I asked who wanted to be a priest?
A boy raised his hand and I asked that he see me outside.
He asked, "Why can't I be a priest?"
Well, at that time, the priests didn't care for (word inaudible) in the seminary.
I didn't think he was intellectually capable.
Later, he said to me, "You didn't leave me flat. You worked on me until I got a chance to go the seminary."
He went to Canada to the seminary.
He went to the ordination with another Capuchin seminarian that was White.
He came to celebrate his 25th anniversary of his ordination.
He dropped dead there. He died of a massive heart attack and stroke.

                                        Sister Audrey

145

FELICIAN SISTERS OF SACRED HEART

Felician Sisters Motherhouse
Livonia, MI

Pictures taken in 2004

Sister Bernardine

Sister Harold

Sister Dolores Ann (Cabrini)

Sister Arthur

Sister Bertha

Sister Elaine, Archivist

Sister Fidelis

Sister Audrey

Sister Stephanie

Sister Leonette

Poetry Of A Parishioner

We are grateful to Cynthia Henderson for allowing us to include two of her unpublished poems. Her poetry speaks to the strength required of survivors of the Black Diaspora.

RISING

Rising
Up in rain rising
Up like Venus from the water
Bearing both shoulders
Straight
Rising head tilted to the sun
Tall-seeming and swaybacked
Full mellow face of the moon goddess
Rising up in foam clouds
Over the big iron cauldron
In her backyard and stirring
White folk's dirty linen
In lye soap and water
Rising up from under
All the cast-iron kettles
It takes to fill the cauldron
Soak the clothes in cool water
Pumped pumped up from the well
Borne kettle by kettle
All the cast iron kettles it takes to
Fill the cauldron
Rinse rinse away the seething
Filth with cool water
Rising up from under
Kettle after cast iron kettle
Popping out huge veins
Behind her honey smooth knees
Reddening in raw patches
Blanching where the lye burns
Up rising up in clouds of clean

Steam up to the foot of
Vulcan's lookout
Over his iron-red valley of a forge
Up head tilted up
Into baskets of clean
Flat-ironed linen smooth
And still warm
Head tilted high
And proud beneath her burden
She rises up the road
The long dusty path into the hills
Past the grayboard shacks
Of the savage ladies like her mama
Who washed nobody's linen but her own
But she rises
Steady-eyed and proud beneath her burden
Up the hill
To the big white-columned houses
Of the fine white gentlemen
Her father's brothers
Who moved up on the hill
In their long low cars
To their pine-paneled dens
And their pale pure ladies
Too delicate to rise in the morning
To deny their own kind
The right to rise
But she rises
Up out of dust and foam
Head tilted high
And proud beneath her burden
Up through spume white clouds
Rising like Venus from the water
Glorious as the red sun rising
Violet and rose in the morning.

March 18, 1977
Cynthia Henderson

COLORED

He is a gray man
And he speaks
The English of the king
With the same burr
As the redheads he scorns.

He is a gray man
But his natural marcelle and
His tropic flowered shirts
Make white men see him olive

He is a gray man
With a pecan-colored wife
Their yellow babies tan
To honey brown
And call themselves
Black

October 1975
Cynthia Henderson

Images From St. Peter Claver

FIRST COMMUNICANTS
And
KNIGHTS OF ST. PETER CLAVER
CIRCA 1937

The two photos from the archives of St. Peter Claver
give us some insight into the time.

In the picture at the top, Ada Maxwell is front row center.
In the picture below, Ada's father is second row, third from right.

153

SACRED HEART CONTINUES
TO
NURTURE ITS LEGACY

Singing & Playing

Administering the
Sacraments

Acknowleding the
Power of the Word

Welcoming the
Children

Feeding the Hungry

Providing Services

Sharing Love

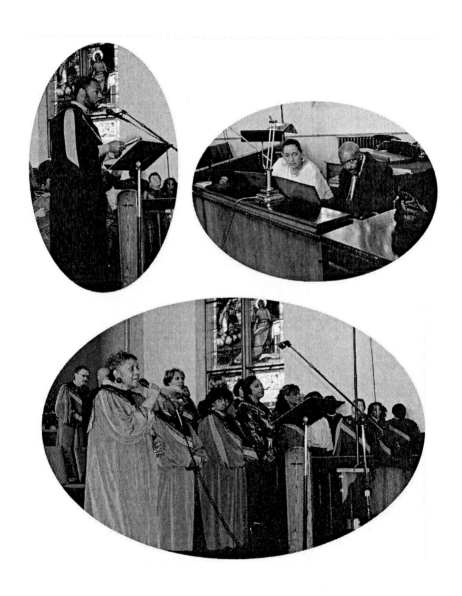

157

159

163

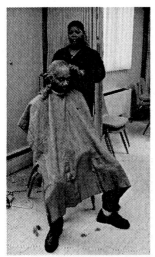

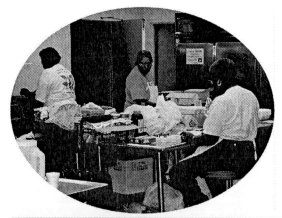

Michaela Terrell

ARTISTS
OF
SACRED HEART

The late John Lynch

Walter Joseph Williams, Jr.

The Sacred Heart buildings and grounds, as
well as this book, have benefited from the
artists shown here.

Additional Interviews

Introduction

The legacy of Sacred Heart is a story of people. The church, the parish house, the activities building, the school and convent (both demolished) are visible structures of the past and present. It is the people that give meaning and purpose to these structures. The story is always about the people and our relationship to God's Word.

Therefore, we wish to include the portions of the interviews recorded in preparation for the "Legacy of Sacred Heart". Many of the interviewees have been quoted in the book by the author to reinforce and attend the messages contained in the text. We are adding others who also shared their stories from the past and present Sacred Heart. Even one line of an interview reflects a thought that is important to both the speaker and the story. There are countless other people, memories, stories and events that are not included in this book. Some day, more can be told and written because the story of Sacred Heart is a living legacy not yet finished.

Father Norman Thomas

Interviewers

Judith Carty
Barbara Hunt
Carole Lasker
Aubrey Lynch
Barbara K. Hughes Smith, Ph.D.
Angela Tarrant-Cook
Michaela Terrell

ADDITIONAL INTERVIEWS

Adams	Maxine	I graduated from Sacred Heart in 1947. The nuns helped to develop the talents of the students. Sacred Heart still provides opportunities for developing each person's talent.
Allen	Harold	I was in Kindergarten at St. Peter Claver. Then we moved to Sacred Heart when I was in the First Grade.
Allen	Mary K. Shanks	At Sacred Heart, we receive the true spirit of holy days by worshipping with our parish family.
Anderson	LaVette	My mother and grandmother were very active here. Now, I try to do some of those things.
Bailey	Zanola	This is my home. My father, Bruce Bailey, was affectionately called "Bishop Bailey." He was one of the first Ministers of Faith.
Barnes	Jacqueline	Father Thomas brings the best out of me. He makes each one of us feel special.

Barrow	Tyrone	When you go to other churches, all you hear is begging for money. Not at Sacred Heart!
Bates-Gresham	Erma	As a young Baptist girl, I came to Sacred Heart for dances, parties and girl scouts.
Bell	Edward	Sacred Heart is where I found Jesus, so this church is for me.
Blount	Erica	I am twelve years old. I think Sacred Heart is a fun place to be. It is a church where you can get involved in some organization. My father, Eric Blount, is one of the Ministers of Faith. He is in charge of the altar servers and I am one of them. Sacred Heart has taught me new things such as the liturgical cycles and reading the Bible. My father prepares me for Sunday Mass by discussing the readings with me.
Bond	Christine	I love my Sacred Heart family.

Bond	Julian	When I was a boy, I used to go to the church all of the time with my grandmother, but didn't know the significance. I'm just now realizing how special a church Sacred Heart really is. I thank my grandmother first and foremost for her kindness and love and for her bringing me back to this great and kind church.
Borders	Brenda	My family has been a part of Sacred Heart since St. Peter Claver days. I love being here.
Boykins	Lorraine	I went to Sacred Heart School for six months. My mother sent me here to straighten me out. Sacred Heart has helped me through some hard times. Father Thomas is always there.

Brathwaite	Cyril	My family is from Trinidad. There are many West Indians at Sacred Heart. My godparents were from Guiana. The West Indian Social League was near Sacred Heart. The group sat around drinking coffee and talking politics. I loved the fellowship there and now at Sacred Heart. My wife and I had heard about Sacred Heart. When we came, something connected for us. We talked to Father Thomas. He was so down to earth. He gave a message to which I could relate. His lessons keep us here.
Bryant	Marvie	We were looking for a Church home. Father Thomas made us feel that we belong.
Burton	Bettie	I do everything I can do to facilitate the ongoing spirit of Sacred Heart.
Butler	Deidre	Father knows all about me and my family. I was born in this church.
Cayruth	Elesia	The homeless are being fed. This must be a good place.

Clark	Betty	I feel the "aliveness" of the spirit every time I come to Sacred Heart.
Clark	Janis	I remember Lucille Crawford playing the organ. And I remember going to St. Peter Claver Community Center Day Care.
Collins	Celia	In order to pay our tuition, my aunt worked for the sisters in the convent daily. My father drove for them. All of us would come every Saturday to clean the furniture and floors in the basement. My aunt was very religious. I remember seeing her fasting, both food and drink. That solidified my faith.
Collins	Kwame	My mother makes me go to church, but there is something for everyone, even me.
Cornish	Cheryl	My husband brought me back to Sacred Heart. This is a church for families, for everybody.

Cornish	LeRoy	I started at St. Peter Claver School, then we moved down here to Sacred Heart. Sister Bernadette directed us in the choir. We went to church before we went to school. I was an altar boy and we went to church seven days a week. We had to shine the wooden floors in school with our Silvercup bread wrappers.
Cosey	Robert	The social side of this congregation is as important as the music to me. The choir members love to party. This camaraderie has caused me to hang on. I am involved with the Administration Committee and the Management Team which looks over repairs and expenditures. We recently completed a tuck-pointing project. The next project is the new roof. The money comes from the collections.
Crispell	Charles	I enjoy working on different committees and driving the church van.
Crumby	James	Mr. Moore was maintenance man in school. We liked him. He was nice to us.

Currie	Dorothy	I remember having breakfast after Sunday Mass in the "corner house" where the nuns used to stay.
Currie	Robert	When I was a child, Mr. Hightower let me sing in the choir.
Davis	Margaret	In 1950, I started to go to St. Peter Claver Community Center on Eliot and Beaubien. It was run by the League of Catholic Women. Hazel Braxton and Theresa Maturen were the directors. I was baptized at Sacred Heart in 1951. Even though I do not live close, I still come because of friends and just the feeling here. I have not felt that way in any other church I have gone to or visited.

Day	Hugh Lee	My desire to marry Audrey Street, now deceased, caused me to become Catholic. She had grown up in the Brewster Projects. She attended St. Peter Claver Community Center and Sacred Heart Church and School. She credited that experience with making her the good woman she became. Audrey loved Father Thomas as the best priest she ever had. He is approachable, friendly, a social activist, humorous and an easy person to talk to regardless of the subject.
Few	Clifton	I have many pleasant memories.
Few	Constance	My husband and I were married by Father Thiefels on October 28, 1946.
Fields	Frank	I became a Catholic through Pat Crispell who was my next door neighbor. My sisters and family have been here a long time now and we will always be here. My mother and father migrated here in the late 1950's due to the factory boom. I really appreciate Father Thomas' homilies and how he relates the Bible to the world.

Fouche	David	I learn something about daily life when I hear the sermon at Sacred Heart.
Fouche	Dominique	I like coming because everybody is nice here.
Fouche	Jodi	We have a good First Communion teacher.
Fouche	Kim	Our four children were all baptized here. We have been here for about twenty-five years.
Fouche	Sabrina	We love people a lot here.
Fouche	Sydney	The people are friendly and you feel welcome when you come in the door.
Gaither	Linda L.	I came to Sacred Heart for the first time with my husband Amos, now deceased. We sat in the back so we could leave early. Amos said, "I never seen nothin' like this." We talked to Father Thomas and became members in June. Amos became a Minister of Service right away.

Gaydu	Serge	I took the responsibility for maintaining the grounds and buildings after Mr. Moore died.
Gilmore	Johnie Mae	I contribute some of my desire to become a member of Sacred Heart to the dynamic teachings of Father Thomas. But, the love, joy and devotion I have seen in my brother, Levon Peoples, played the greatest role in my decision to worship here. I felt the best way to achieve the love, inner happiness, peace and joy that Levon demonstrated would start with worship at Sacred Heart.
Grays	Reginald	My grandmother, Mamie Grays, and my aunt, Gladys Grays were here. I have been coming to Sacred Heart since I was 7 years old. We would be at church all day long. I remember running around Father's house while my grandmother and auntie fixed breakfast. My roots are here. There is love here and everyone is welcoming and cares.
Gregory	Rose Virginia	For 40 years, I've been a member of Sacred Heart. My heart, my soul, my life is Sacred Heart.

Guillean	Elysia	This church is special to me. I just really like it. Father Thomas talks about Jesus.
Guillean	Theresa	I come here because I want my daughter to grow up knowing a loving God.
Gunn	Barbara	It is important that we show that we care about each other.
Hamilton-Lucas	Mary Grace	My aunt, Louise Harris, was one of the first black students to go to school here. She looked white, very fair. It was the light-skinned blacks that were in school while it was still German. The nuns were mean. They treated the colored students with an indifference. The students knew they weren't welcome.
Harris	Vickie	I talk about Sacred Heart all of the time. When my mother comes to visit, we always come here. My kids ask, "Aren't we going to church today?" And they are teenagers. You know that's remarkable.
Hazley	Candace	My wedding at Sacred Heart was the most personal and special event of my life.

Hazley	Nellie	This church gives love. I cried when I first came. I love the choir and Father Thomas and I enjoy working with the Youth Liturgical Dancers who help us pray through dance.
Henton	Beatrice	I was sent to Sacred Heart in the 1950's because I was black. I had been going to St. George. It was all black, but it closed. I went to Catholic schools because I felt safe. My neighborhood was rough. I begged my parents to let me stay at Sacred Heart. It was hard for my parents to pay tuition. Also, we didn't have a gym or enough typewriters, except for the seniors. We walked to the old St. Peter Claver building for gym. I attended Sacred Heart after the school closed, but when I got married, I started having children one after the other. My husband was in the military and it was hard. The church would not let us use birth control, so I left Sacred Heart.

Hogan	Beverly	I came to Sacred Heart with my sister, Leslie Morgan, a year after they closed a lot of churches down. I was a single mother with four children. It is such a supportive church. Father Thomas knows his parishioners by name. My first reaction was, "Is this a Catholic Church?" I was used to quiet churches.
Hope	Gay	I come here and help clean up because Sacred Heart helps me.
Howard	Connie	I came to Sacred Heart in 1945. The school had many plays that took place in Brewster Center. Later years, when I came back to Sacred Heart, I knew I would never leave again.
Hunt	Barbara	Originally, I wanted to leave Sacred Heart School because I didn't like the nuns. I'm back now and I love it.
Jenkins	Diamond	I like coming to church.

Jennings	Mary Frances	I remember being in awe of the nuns who seemed other worldly and mystical. Then, I was taken under the wing of Sister Humilitas who humanized me. She fostered my development and facilitated my first employment. I now reside in Nevada, but Sacred Heart will always be a parish family to which I belong.
Johnson	Sandgenetta	I joined the St. Vincent de Paul Society to help others. That's what Sacred Heart people do.
Lee	Lillian	The feeling here is overwhelming. It opens avenues for me to live a better life.
Livingston	Andrea	I joined the Choir, Karate, Ministers and Dancers. I love everything about Sacred Heart.
Lofton	Michael	Father Thomas gives me the spiritual feeling that I need for life.
Louis-Wilson	Leslie	When I was not in church, Father noticed and asked me, "Where have you been?"

Love	Kathy	Three of us are telling this story, my mother Kathy Love, her friend, Beatrice Cooper and myself. We were church shopping. I recalled that my Cameroonian friends felt welcome at Sacred Heart. I told my mother and Beatrice, "Come go to the get-down church with me!" Mama initially refused to set foot in a Catholic Church. She said, "My mother would roll over in her grave!" When she relented, we went and I still remember feeling a Spirit of Love when we walked in the door. Mama smiled approvingly. Bea and I said we couldn't believe that there are drums and a tambourine in a Catholic Church. The black, red and green altar curtains invited me. I could see the love Father Thomas had for his flock. Now, when the church doors open, we want to be in there.
Lucas	Tomika	I came with my husband. Sacred Heart is totally different. There is more SOUL!
March	Robecca	I don't know where I would be without the guidance I receive at Sacred Heart.

Maxwell	Thomas	I was best man at Cyril Brathwaite's wedding. I hadn't been here in 15 years. Father Thomas said, "Hi Thomas." I was amazed. Father Thomas' leadership is what draws people.
McAlister	Wilbert	I feel comfortable working here with such a supportive and diverse group.
McCall	Louise Williams	I was baptized at St. Mary's and went to Sacred Heart in the fifth grade.
McCauley	Philip Henry	I remember that dad was in the Knights of St. Peter Claver. It was a very active organization.
McCloud	Paris	Father Thomas, as a visiting pastor, baptized me at St. Patrick's. I followed him to Sacred Heart. He plays a good role. After school, I was home for a minute, but instead of hanging out, I'd come across Chrysler to the church until Father Thomas got tired of looking at me – but he never told me that. He would go to the projects to get his hair cut, even after the riots, and take the kids in the neighborhood to play hockey.

McGhee	Elaine	Our father would not allow my twin sister, Eunice Stiger, and me to go to public schools. That's why we went to Sacred Heart. The closeness of the children and our relationship with the nuns was unique. We had all black students, so we were very conscious of our heritage. My dad was the basketball coach. In 1946, SH won the championship and received a huge trophy.
McKinnon	Gloria	My neighbor, Elouise Thomas-Johnson, invited me to Sacred Heart. On December 18, 1983, I was baptized. Carole Lasker gave me my first bible and I still have it. Since then, I have become a Minister of Faith and belong to a lot of groups. I can't see myself any place else.
McNeal-Lett	Gwendolyn F.	We don't come here to dress up. I come for the foundation, someone to lean on.
Moore	Denese	Whether you are from the suburbs or from around the corner, you are welcome here.

Morgan	Jenario	I really like Sacred Heart for a lot of reasons. The membership is diverse, both economically and ethnically. They embrace all and appear to feel real good about the church and church ownership. They have completely adopted Vatican II. Sacred Heart really typifies what Vatican II is about, that is, everybody interfacing with their faith and taking responsibility in their parish.
Morgan	Leslie	My father died the same month that St. Theresa's closed. We were trying to find a place to have his funeral. I had met Father Thomas at a gathering about church closings. I called to ask about having the funeral there. Father Thomas said, "Sure." The community really reached out to our family and that impressed me.
Murphy	Loretta	Sacred Heart is my "feeding ground." It is the source of strength for my life since ninth grade.
Ogundipe	Justina	My husband talked to someone at work who said, "Go to Sacred Heart!"

Ogundipe	Stephen	I was baptized in Nigeria. The Mass at Sacred Heart is very much like my experience in Africa.
Palkowski	Delphine	My first Sacred Heart experience was astounding. It was in the old school building in the Alcoholic Center run by Father Quinn. It was a "casual Mass." It blew me away. I was flabbergasted. I didn't know if it was wonderful or horrible. But, it was exceedingly thought provoking. Being a family member at Sacred Heart spoils one.
Pate	Carol Ann Fallings	I went to Sacred Heart from the first to eighth grades. There were many children from the projects. Sister Janet, third grade, made gifts for the children. I moved back from Iowa several years ago. I live outside Flint, an hour drive, so I am not here every Sunday, but I come back just because of the peace of mind here. When Father Thomas speaks, he is not just talking to us, but is walking the walk with us.

Peterson	Harriette	I love the spiritual growth, the activities, the volunteer opportunities provided at Sacred Heart.
Robinson	Natalia	I'm glad that my grandmother, Virginia Robinson, and my mother brought me to Sacred Heart.
Seay	Constance	My sister and I had to cross Hastings Street when we went to school here. The neighborhood had a lot of businesses, stores and restaurants. It was working families that lived in the projects. Most of them had migrated from the South. We lived in the projects until we got established and moved out. We went to St. Peter Claver after school because our mother was working.

Seay	Gwen	I went to Sacred Heart from the first to the eighth grade in the 1950's. No matter where we moved, we always came here. Mom was active in school. If my sister and I got in trouble, we prayed that mom wouldn't know. We passed several public schools to go to Sacred Heart. My parents liked the discipline and the smaller number of students. Even when people move away, they come here when they are in town.
Sheehan	Jim	Integration and segregation are different issues in the North than in the South. Black people in the city did not know whites and vice versa. That is a major problem and needs to be addressed. I worked with Father Thomas when I was with the Human Relations Office. I left the priesthood and came here with my wife and daughter for the experience, for integration. Sacred Heart is socially active. The big attraction is that you can be committed to a cause and belong here.

Smith	Barbara K. Hughes	In 1985, two life-changing incidents shattered my life. My father died without warning and my husband abandoned me and my children from my first marriage. After months of grieving, I decided to pray for the return of my husband and received counseling from Father Thomas. He named me "Hope,' was non-judgmental and encouraged me to seek God. In the end, it was my grief that saved me. The more I hurt, the closer my walk became with God.
Smith	Sandra Richardson	The energy at Sacred Heart attracted so many young people, including those from the Brewster Projects. I met my husband there. Soon, a group of us formed "The Under Thirty Group." The sole purpose of the group was to educate and heighten the cultural awareness of the young sisters and brothers living in the Brewster Projects.
Sowell-Bradley	Patricia	The first day I came to Sacred Heart, the Holy Spirit whispered to me, "You're home." I haven't gone anywhere since.

Spivey	Bessie	I like to be at Sacred Heart with people who are nurturing and who get along.
Stiger	Eunice	I left the Church because I married a divorced man. The Church would not allow my two sons to be baptized. Everyone knows how Father Thomas accepts everybody. That's why I rejoined Sacred Heart after so many years. My twin sister, Elaine McGhee, and I still continue the relationships we had when we went to Sacred Heart.
Sykes	Carolyn Tobias	Beginning in 1946, I came by streetcar and bus from the North-end to Sacred Heart School. We liked the nuns, even though some of them were rough. They taught you well. If you behaved, you did not have a problem.
Tarrant	Geralyn	Sacred Heart is an example of what all churches should be.
Tarrant	Mawasi	There's so much to do here. I like the Christmas and Halloween parties.

Tarrant-Cook	Angela M.	Everything here reminds me of the Gospels. Father Thomas is our "Good Shepherd."
Tate	Stephen	I attended Sacred Heart from the second to the ninth grades. The nuns really cared about the kids. When Sacred Heart had to close some of the grades, some of the nuns shed tears. The education was excellent.
Thomas-Johnson	Elouise	The first time I came to Sacred Heart, I knew this was where I am supposed to be.
Thompson	Herbert	We used to meet in the "corner house" like one big, happy family.
Thorne	John F.	Father wants me to start a youth ministry here, so I am coming "home."
Thorne	John	Community activism was one of the things that attracted me to Sacred Heart.
Turner-Motley	Patricia	I came in 1994. It is warm and comfortable here. This is my "home church."

Vandergift	Dorothy	The first thing that drew me in was the "kiss of peace." It was so wonderful! I love the way the Word of the Lord is presented by Father Thomas.
Vassallo	Marianna	In October of 2002, Eva Ray was my patient at Harper Hospital. I kidded Eva that I was a recovering Catholic. I need music to feed my soul. I liked to go to churches with a gospel choir. Eva told me that I should come to Sacred Heart. I went the following Sunday. Then, I went back to the hospital and gave Eva a big hug. I became a parishioner a few months later.
Walker	Andre	You are not a stranger here. When you come to the door, you're a part of the church family. I never feel out of place here.
Walker	Ashleigh (King)	If you are feeling a little sad, you can come here and it will lift you up. It's great!
Walker	D'Andre	I've been here my whole life. Even if you are a sinner, you can worship here.

Walker	Devin	I come to this church because I learn about God in my First Communion class.
Walker	Jerry (King)	I come with my parents. I enjoy singing in the youth choir.
Walker	Leigh	Even if I leave for awhile, I am always welcomed back.
Wallace	Evelyn	I came to Sacred Heart for the first time in the '70's. I could only come once a month because I was working, but I wanted my children to come. Father Thomas set me up with a family that would bring my children to church. My grandchildren and my great grandchildren have since been brought up at Sacred Heart.
Wardlaw	Lillie Belle M.	I started at Sacred Heart in 1933 when it was still a German and Italian parish. I was a member at St. Peter Claver, but attended Sacred Heart School. I was put into Sacred Heart because I was always getting into devilment at Lincoln Elementary. All of the kids at Sacred Heart, whether German or Italian or black got along and had lots of fun. There were 5 black students in my graduating class of 1937.

Washington	Larry	I came to Sacred Heart in 1995. I was homeless, hungry and needing help. I had never been to a Catholic Church before. Sometimes, my family wouldn't know where I was. But, I still kept coming to Sacred Heart.
Watson	Avis Carey	I went to a Baptist Church, but I was afraid and nervous because of the fire and brimstone sermons. I went to St. Rose before they tore it down. My mother asked if I was afraid at the Catholic Mass. I said, "No," so my mother had me baptized Catholic. My mother started working closely with the nuns and encouraged me.
Watts	Michelle	There's a ribbon of peace that flows through the church. Tuesday Mass is so special.

Williams	Martha Mary Lee	My family has been Catholic for generations. My family's slave owner was Catholic. In Detroit, we first went to St. Peter Claver (SPC) which was a mission parish. The Knights of St. Peter Claver would watch guard over the deceased Knights who were kept at home until the funeral. SPC was ethnically diverse with a large number from Jamaica and the West Indies. The church was small, but I remember the large families that attended like the Walkers and the Greenhouses. The entire Walker family had beautiful, bird-like voices. Ursula Walker is well known and still sings in Detroit.
Wilson	Brittany	I like coming to Sacred Heart. I like being involved in the Liturgical Dance Ministry.
Wilson	Regina	Father Thomas was right there with me during some hard times. I love Sacred Heart.
Woodland	Denise	Father Thomas is my godfather and mentor. He inspires me to do my best always.

Wyche	Gladis	When I first came with Sue Mercer, I had an overwhelming sense of warmth.